Praise for *Making AI Work for Britain: From Strategies to Practice*

'The UK sits at a pivotal point in its potential as an AI superpower. Professor Brown has superbly captured the challenge of turning opportunity and ambition into reality, eloquently providing a roadmap to success. Government should step up and listen, or it will risk irrelevancy in this new world. We need more ambition like this.'

— **Air Cdre (Ret'd) J B Crawford CBE,**
Former Commandant, Air and Space Warfare Centre

'This book provides a thoughtful framework for asking the right questions about how Britain turns AI ambition into real-world impact.'

— **Lord Ranger of Northwood**

'Across financial services and public data infrastructure alike, the UK excels at admiring the AI opportunity. This book does something rarer: it asks what realistic delivery actually looks like, and what has to change to make it happen.'

— **Samantha Seaton**, Co-Chair, UK Smart Data Council

'Written on a bedrock of research and experience, Alan Brown's *Making AI Work for Britain* is a complete and clear guide to the AI revolution. The book introduces the great opportunity AI provides to successfully navigate the next big step in digital transformation and offers an important roadmap for what the UK should do next. I highly recommend it to anyone thinking about AI strategy.'

— **Dave West**, CEO, Scrum.org

'Alan draws on insights from digital transformation to identify how to introduce AI effectively into business and government. One of the most compelling visions is of AI assurance as an export industry.'

— **Professor John A McDermid OBE FREng,**
Institute for Safe Autonomy, University of York

‘At a time of relentless digital disruption, this book focuses on the hardest problem of all: institutional change. Brown explains why AI exposes the limits of existing structures, and how organisations must fundamentally rethink how they govern, decide and deliver.’

— **Tony Moretta**, CEO, Digital Jersey

‘Professor Brown offers an optimistic yet pragmatic and realistic blueprint for a future national debate around how AI can reshape the future of our economy. The book provides policymakers and business leaders with a roadmap that creates a pathway to achieve the UK’s AI ambitions.’

— **Tristan Wilkinson**, Engagement Director, Mozaic

‘This is an excellent overview of the issues facing the UK in governing AI, developing the AI sector, growing the economy in an AI age, and integrating AI ethically and effectively into business and government. It lays out clearly all the areas to which government and industry need to pay close attention – where there are no complete answers, conclusions, or outcomes. I will be using this guide to key issues for my own research and policy work.’

— **Simeon Yates**, Professor of Digital Culture,
University of Liverpool

‘Professor Brown’s well-researched book provides valuable insight for the informed lay reader wanting to understand more on AI’s impact in the UK. It offers a clear perspective on the UK’s current AI strategy and strengths in both a historical and global setting.’

— **Dr Louise Bennett**, Digital Policy Alliance Advisory Board

‘This book offers well-founded advice, innovative ideas and practical steps to help leaders and their advisers drive effective action in making AI work for the nation’

— **Professor Edward Rochead FIMA, AFWES,**
Chair of the Alliance for Data Science Professionals

‘A timely, pragmatic, clear-eyed analysis of the UK’s AI landscape. Successfully shifts the conversation from abstract technological hype toward the gritty, institutional realities of implementation.’

— **Chad Bond**, Strategy and Innovation Director, Zaizi

Making AI Work for Britain

Making AI Work for Britain

From Strategies to Practice

Alan W. Brown

LONDON PUBLISHING PARTNERSHIP

Published by London Publishing Partnership
www.londonpublishingpartnership.co.uk

ISBN: 978-1-916749-67-2 (pbk)
ISBN: 978-1-916749-68-9 (iPDF)
ISBN: 978-1-916749-69-6 (epub)
ISBN: 978-1-916749-71-9 (Open Access)

A catalogue record for this book is
available from the British Library

This book has been composed in Candara

Images used in the figures were designed
by Freepik

Copy-edited and typeset by
T&T Productions Ltd, London
www.tandtproductions.com

Printed and bound in Great Britain
by Hobbs the Printers Ltd

Contents

Foreword

The United Kingdom has never lacked ambition when it comes to technology. For decades we have produced world-class research, pioneering companies and a vibrant ecosystem of innovation. Artificial intelligence is no exception. From our universities to our start-ups, Britain remains one of the most dynamic environments in the world for developing AI.

Yet, as Professor Alan Brown highlights in *Making AI Work for Britain*, there is an uncomfortable gap between ambition and execution.

The UK is producing no shortage of AI strategies, road maps and policy frameworks. But the real challenge now is far more practical: how do we ensure AI is actually adopted, embedded and used to deliver meaningful outcomes for the country?

This book arrives at an important moment because it shifts the conversation from aspiration to implementation. Professor Brown argues that the primary barriers to AI adoption are not technological but institutional. The same structural issues that have slowed large-scale transformation across parts of government – complex procurement processes, fragmented accountability, gaps in capability and limited coordination – can easily prevent the effective deployment of AI as well.

In that sense, culture and institutions may matter more than the technology itself. Technology can be built, bought or accessed. Skills can be developed. Infrastructure can be improved. But unless organizations are prepared to change how they operate, even the most powerful technologies will struggle to deliver real value. Strategy documents alone do not transform countries; institutions and leadership do. This is why the book's focus on implementation is particularly valuable.

Too often debates about AI become centred on the technology itself – its potential, its risks and the frameworks required to regulate it. These are important conversations but governments in particular must guard against focusing so heavily on the technology that they lose sight of the outcomes it is meant to serve.

The key question should not simply be 'How do we use AI?' It should be 'What outcomes do we want to achieve – and how can AI help us deliver them?'

Whether the objective is improving productivity, modernizing public services, supporting economic growth or enabling better policy decisions, AI should be viewed as a tool that helps achieve clearly defined national goals.

Professor Brown's call for stronger institutional coordination around AI adoption across government is therefore a welcome contribution to the debate. Transformation rarely happens through advisory committees alone; it requires clear ownership and the authority to act.

Equally important is the emphasis placed on the machinery of implementation. Procurement systems must be capable of commissioning innovative solutions. Data infrastructure must be treated as strategic national capability rather than routine IT housekeeping. And public servants must develop the practical skills required not only to understand AI but also to commission, evaluate and oversee its use responsibly.

Awareness alone is not capability. Adoption requires expertise.

Another valuable insight in this book is the need to learn from sectors beyond government. Many industries – from finance to manufacturing and logistics – have already been integrating advanced technologies into complex operational environments. Their experience offers important lessons about how organizations adapt, manage risk and build the internal capacity required to adopt new technologies successfully.

AI adoption in the UK will ultimately depend on the strength of the wider ecosystem in which government, academia and industry work together.

At the same time, we should recognize that AI remains a rapidly evolving field. The pace of innovation is extraordinary and the societal implications are still unfolding. That makes open and thoughtful debate not only useful but necessary.

Professor Brown's book makes an important contribution to this discussion. By focusing on the practical realities of implementation, it challenges policymakers and leaders to move beyond aspiration and address the institutional changes required to make AI work in practice. It reminds us that the real test of any strategy lies not in the document itself, but in the outcomes it enables.

This book does not claim to provide all the answers. Nor should it. The transformation that AI represents is too significant and too complex for any single blueprint to resolve. But it does provide something equally important: a thoughtful framework for asking the right questions about how Britain turns AI ambition into real-world impact.

If it succeeds in prompting a more practical and outcomes-focused debate about AI adoption in the UK, it will have served a valuable purpose.

LORD KULVEER RANGER

Preface

For more than twenty years, we have seen the United Kingdom navigate successive waves of digital transformation: from e-government initiatives to fintech innovation, from NHS digitalization to the current surge in artificial intelligence. Each wave has brought real promise through efficiency gains, expanded access to services and new economic opportunities. Yet each has also revealed persistent gaps between ambition and delivery, between headline announcements and experience on the ground, and between the capabilities of our best institutions and the needs of those left behind.

The UK possesses exceptional assets for AI leadership: world-class researchers, innovative companies, experienced civil servants and deep expertise across sectors from finance to healthcare. Yet we repeatedly fall short of realizing the transformative potential these assets represent. The question central to this work is not whether the UK can lead in AI, but whether it has the institutional wisdom, cultural courage and authentic commitment to inclusion to do so in a way that strengthens rather than fractures business and society.

It is a necessary conversation. The UK is at a critical strategic crossroads – not a single path forward but a choice between fundamentally different approaches, each with distinct consequences. One road follows the US model, which prioritizes speed, accepts platform dependency on a small number of hyperscale providers and relies on market forces to distribute benefits. A second follows the EU model, which prioritizes citizen protection through comprehensive regulation, accepting slower adoption and higher compliance costs. A third, and the one this book argues the UK is best placed to pursue, is an adaptive path: building sovereign capability in areas that matter most, setting governance standards that others adopt and using the UK's distinctive institutional assets (from the NHS to the City of London) as proving grounds for AI that is both innovative and accountable.

These are not abstract alternatives. They are being decided now, through hundreds of procurement decisions, infrastructure investments and regulatory choices that individually appear pragmatic but collectively constitute a strategic direction. The UK's choices over the next three to five years will shape not only its competitive position but also its ability to embed ethical principles, build inclusive opportunities and sustain public trust in digital systems.

The argument that strategy is what gets implemented rather than what gets declared is not new. Henry Mintzberg made the case decades ago; in his framing, realized strategy emerges from patterns of action, not from documents of intent. More recently, Mariana Mazzucato has argued, with growing evidence, that governments have hollowed out their implementation capacity by outsourcing to consultancies, creating organizations that can commission transformation but not deliver it – and that cannot learn from what they commission. These points are well made.

This book's contribution is not in general insights but in specific evidence: that the UK's digital transformation failures share a common structural pattern, recurring across two decades and multiple administrations, and that AI will reproduce this pattern unless the institutional architecture changes. The five reform strands proposed in the third part of this book are designed to break that cycle – not by adding new strategy documents to the pile, but by changing the governance, procurement, skills, infrastructure and accountability mechanisms through which strategy becomes (or fails to become) practice.

At its simplest, the lesson of the UK's most successful digital reform can be expressed in a simple way: consolidate demand, diversify supply. The Government Digital Service worked because it coordinated what government bought through common platforms, standards and spend controls, while opening the supplier base to competition. For AI, the UK is in danger of inverting this formula. Supply has concentrated into a handful of US and Chinese AI foundation model providers while demand for AI tools and services remains fragmented across departments, organizations and institutions. Much of what follows in this book is an argument for correcting that inversion.

Unfortunately, the conversation about the UK's AI choices remains fragmented. Policymakers focus on regulation and competitiveness, business leaders on innovation and growth, civil society on risks and equity, and technologists on capability building. Each perspective contains vital truths, but the silos they exist in prevent the integrated thinking that successful transformation requires. This book attempts to bridge these divides. It argues that governance, skills, ethics, innovation and inclusion are not competing priorities but interdependent dimensions of a coherent strategy. It suggests that if a nation with the UK's democratic traditions, technical capabilities and institutional depth cannot chart a course that delivers both innovation and accountability, then this raises profound questions about whether such a synthesis is possible at all.

The analysis draws on more than two decades of work across government reform, organizational change and sector transformation, as well as on conversations with dozens of practitioners, policymakers and front line workers who experience digital change where it matters most. The result is a book written primarily for UK policymakers and government leaders who shape the institutional landscape, and for organizational leaders in business, public agencies and civil society who must translate national strategy into local reality.

To achieve its goals, the book follows a three-part sequence.

- 'Part I: What Got Us Here' examines the UK's digital history, not for its own sake, but to identify the patterns of success and failure that will determine whether AI adoption succeeds or stalls. The UK has been through several waves of digital transformation. Each has produced legitimate achievements and instructive failures. The same structural barriers (fragmented governance, inadequate procurement and the separation of technology design from policy design) have recurred across decades and sectors. Understanding these patterns is not optional background; it is the essential foundation for avoiding their being repeated.

- 'Part II: What Matters Now' turns to the present: the institutional, workforce and governance challenges that must be addressed in the near term, before path dependencies lock in. It examines the gap between the UK's AI ambitions and what institutions can deliver, diagnoses the systemic barriers that cause this gap, and identifies the specific reforms to institutions, skills, ethics and risk governance that would close it.

- 'Part III: What Comes Next' locates the UK in the global landscape and makes the case for a distinctive strategic path. It assesses the competing international models the UK could emulate, argues for an adaptive path that plays to the UK's strengths and sets out the practical steps required to turn strategy into delivery.

Each part builds on the previous one: historical lessons inform current priorities; current priorities shape the strategic choices ahead. Each chapter explains the issues directly, avoids jargon wherever possible and aims to help readers make informed decisions that matter now and will matter in the years ahead.

Readers seeking a consolidated view of the book's recommendations (whether before reading the full argument or after) will find one in chapter 9.

The pathway is not predetermined. But progress is possible if we approach the task ahead with clarity, collaborate across divides and commit to the principle that technology must serve human flourishing. I hope this book serves as both a mirror to understand where we are and a compass for the road ahead.

PART I

WHAT GOT US HERE

CHAPTER 1

AI and the UK digital economy

This chapter sets out why AI represents a qualitatively different phase of technological change, what is new and what stays the same, and why the UK must treat this moment with seriousness and intellectual honesty.

Setting the scene: why AI and why now?

The UK is at a crucial turning point in how it uses digital technology and AI. Recent headlines have focused on rapid innovation and big changes, but, beneath the excitement, many people, including business leaders, policymakers and citizens, are asking what these changes really mean for jobs, power, democracy and everyday life.

This turning point became especially clear in September 2025, as US President Donald Trump's state visit concluded and the UK announced what has been called 'the largest commercial package ever secured during a State Visit'[1]: this includes Microsoft committing £22 billion,[2] Google pledging £5 billion[3] and Nvidia announcing £11 billion[4] in AI infrastructure investments. These announcements, following the January 2025 release of the UK AI Opportunities Action Plan,[5] mark a pivotal moment in which the UK is effectively deciding its place in the global AI order and marking out the path to achieving it.

Announcements of some of the foundation steps have already been made. The North East has been designated as an AI Growth Zone with expectations of £30 billion in investment and promises of more than 5,000 new jobs.[6] Data centres are sprouting across the country. Up to £250 billion has been pledged in cross-Atlantic deals,[7] transforming the UK's AI landscape at unprecedented speed.

Yet headline investment figures and partnership stability are not the same thing. The Technology Prosperity Deal signed in September 2025 was brought into doubt within three months, not over technology disagreements but over the UK's Digital Services Tax, food safety standards and Online Safety Act provisions.[8] The episode illustrates a recurring theme of this book: the gap between aspiration and implementation, between what is announced and what endures.

From AI user to digital sovereignty

As much as the wave of AI investment marks an important breakthrough in the UK's digital story, it also raises complex questions about who controls the UK's digital future. It is now increasingly clear that the UK has to decide not only how much AI it wants to adopt, but how much digital sovereignty it wants to retain.

In this book, 'digital sovereignty' is used to refer to the UK's ability to set and enforce its own rules over the data, compute infrastructure and AI systems that underpin its public services, economy and security. It is not about building everything at home or cutting ties with global partners. Rather, it is about ensuring that when critical systems fail, standards change or abuses occur, UK institutions have the authority, information and tools to respond under UK law and with necessary oversight.

In this regard, three digital sovereignty levers matter most in practice.

1. *Compute power.* This concerns where the high-end infrastructure that trains and runs AI systems is located, who owns and operates it, and which jurisdiction ultimately applies.

2. *Data.* This concerns who governs access to core national datasets in areas such as health, welfare, justice and finance; how critical infrastructure is designed and maintained; and on what terms national assets are shared with private platforms.

3. *System oversight.* This concerns which institutions can audit, pause or reconfigure AI-driven services that directly affect citizens' lives, regardless of whether the underlying technology is foreign or UK owned.

Efforts such as the UK Compute Roadmap and the AI Opportunities Action Plan, alongside new AI Growth Zones across the country, are among the multiple early attempts to build domestic capability, from national supercomputers to regional AI data centres and specialized chips.

However, these are (comparatively) small, embryonic efforts. The multibillion-pound commitments by Microsoft, Google, Nvidia and others bring capital, skills and early access to advanced models that the UK could not realistically replicate alone. They also embed public services, research institutions and businesses more deeply into a small number of hyperscale platforms whose commercial incentives, security priorities and legal obligations are set elsewhere. The strategic question is not 'US or UK?', but to what extent the UK is willing to trade long-term bargaining power and institutional control for short-term acceleration.

Digital sovereignty therefore sits at the heart of the leadership paradoxes that must be faced in defining the UK's AI strategy. The pursuit of innovation and speed through global platforms can dilute the UK's ability to ensure inclusion, safety and fairness on its own terms. Conversely, attempts to build everything domestically risk fragmentation, duplication, and missed opportunities for collaboration and scale. UK leaders should not retreat from global ecosystems, but instead shape them: investing in sovereign compute infrastructure, strengthening data institutions, and giving regulators the mandate and tools to enforce standards on any system that shapes UK citizens' lives.

Reality check: the digital sovereignty trade-off is not reversible

The UK cannot indefinitely defer choices about digital sovereignty while accepting infrastructure investment on terms set by others. Every data centre built under foreign ownership, every critical public service migrated to hyperscale platforms headquartered elsewhere, and every AI system whose training data and algorithms remain proprietary and inaccessible to UK regulators incrementally transfers practical control over the digital infrastructure that underpins national security, economic competitiveness and democratic governance. These are not easily reversible decisions. The computational and financial barriers to switching cloud providers or retraining foundation models at scale mean that today's convenience becomes tomorrow's dependency.

The UK is making choices about digital sovereignty right now through hundreds of procurement decisions, partnership agreements and infrastructure investments. Such choices will constrain policy options for decades. The question is whether these choices are being made strategically and transparently, or whether they are emerging haphazardly from the accumulated decisions of actors who lack awareness of the broader implications.

The choice is straightforward but consequential: accept infrastructure investment on the current terms and gain speed at the cost of embedded dependencies, impose sovereignty conditions and accept negotiation complexity with potential delays or build UK alternatives and trade years of capability for complete control. Each path makes sense under different assumptions about risk tolerance, negotiating leverage and institutional capacity. What does not make sense is pretending the choice is not being made. It is, right now, through accumulated procurement decisions and partnership agreements that individually appear pragmatic but collectively constitute a strategic direction.

Not all AI is the same: a quick practical guide to AI

Before examining the UK's digital foundations, it is important to be precise about what 'AI' means in the context of this book. Different types of AI demand different governance, different procurement, different skills and different risk management. Too often, public debate, policy documents and strategic plans treat 'AI' as a single phenomenon. It is not. At a minimum, three categories matter for strategy.

1. Narrow AI and specialist systems are designed for specific, well-defined tasks: reading medical scans, detecting financial fraud, optimizing logistics, predicting equipment failure and so on. These systems have been in operational use for years, particularly in healthcare, defence and financial services. Their capabilities are bounded, their failure modes are relatively well understood and their value is proven. When a radiology department deploys an AI system that flags potential tumours for human review, that is narrow AI performing a specific task within a defined workflow.

2. Generative AI and large language models (LLMs) are the technologies driving the current public and political interest. Systems such as ChatGPT, Claude and Gemini can generate text, code, images and conversation across an enormous range of topics. Their capabilities are impressive, but their risk profile is fundamentally different from narrow AI. They can 'hallucinate', generating plausible but fabricated information with the same confidence as accurate statements. UK courts have already encountered legal submissions citing case law that does not exist, produced by lawyers who did not understand that LLMs generate probable text, not verified facts.[9] In many organizational settings, LLMs function as expensive substitutes for traditional search capabilities rather than genuinely new capabilities, and emerging evidence suggests they can reduce productivity when deployed without clear protocols for verification and use.[10]

3. AI-as-infrastructure refers to the compute capabilities, data platforms and foundation model layers that underpin both of the above. This is where the sovereignty and governance questions analysed in the previous section are most acute: who owns the data centres, who controls the training data and who sets the terms of access? Decisions made at this layer constrain what is possible at the application layer for decades.

Of course, this is just a broad, simplified categorization. Much more lies beneath the surface.[11] Yet these simple distinctions matter for every aspect of strategy examined in this book. The regulatory framework appropriate for a narrow AI diagnostic tool (where risks are bounded and testable) is quite different from the framework needed for a general-purpose LLM embedded in citizen-facing government services (where risks are emergent and unpredictable). Procurement approaches that work for specialist systems, with clear specifications and measurable outcomes, break down when applied to generative tools whose capabilities and limitations shift with each usage context and every model update. Workforce strategies must equip people to work with both: to trust narrow AI outputs that have been validated, and to verify generative AI outputs that have not.

The analysis throughout this book applies to all three categories, but the reader should be alert to which is under discussion at any given point. Where the distinction matters for a specific argument (and it frequently does) the text will attempt to say so explicitly.

The strengths (and weaknesses) of the UK's digital foundation

Consequently, these new investments are not just about building new technology. They represent a major declaration about the UK's independence and leadership in the AI era. Right now, the UK faces choices about very different paths for its future.

The UK has a strong foundation: it is known particularly as a centre for financial services, for its creative industry, as an established leader in biotech, and for the advanced digital government services it provides to citizens and businesses. However, a new wave of technological change demands further action. The government wants the UK to be an 'AI maker not an AI taker'[12] by creating and leading in AI, not just using AI technology made elsewhere. There are bold investments, new research centres and ambitious regulations. But progress is uneven. While some businesses and regions are thriving, many are struggling to keep up or even survive in this fast-changing environment.

Recent years have shown both the strengths and weaknesses of the UK's digital investments. The Covid-19 pandemic forced rapid changes as remote work, online healthcare, digital education and virtual government services became essential. These pressures revealed where the UK is strong and where it still needs improvement.[13] Leaders saw both the benefits of quick action and the problems caused by old systems, poor procurement practices and slow adaptation.

It also revealed that digital technology now affects every part of society, and how deeply such services are interconnected. For instance, decisions made on how mobile phones collect data can have unexpected impacts on healthcare services. Similarly, mistakes made in a data centre in another country can severely disrupt vital services in the UK. These connections and dependencies are becoming even more apparent as digital services become the norm.

As a result of these experiences, recognition is growing that the UK's opportunity with AI is not just about technology; it is about culture, strategy and people. Success will depend on leaders who know how to use AI effectively, build strong teams, understand technology adoption and take smart risks. The real challenge is how the UK brings together its people, institutions and ideas to deliver meaningful change.

Five paradoxes and key challenges for UK leaders

What have we learned from these digital experiences of the past two decades that will be the basis for the UK's digital future? Perhaps the best way to address this question is to acknowledge that digital transformation has presented UK leaders with a series of intertwined paradoxes. That is, opportunities shadowed by risks, and urgent dilemmas that defy easy resolution. These tensions are shaping every strategic choice, policy debate and implementation road map. As we enter the AI era, recognizing, highlighting and debating these paradoxes is critical.

Paradox 1: innovation versus inclusion

Digital technologies (now headed by AI) promise extraordinary productivity, efficiency and creative potential. Yet, at the same

Figure 1. The five paradoxes facing UK leaders.

time they risk amplifying the digital divide, and leaving behind those regions, sectors and communities without access to the latest technologies or the relevant skills to use them. Leaders face the challenge of driving breakthrough innovation while embedding robust policies for inclusion, equal opportunity and lifelong learning.

The innovation imperative is real. The UK's competitive future depends on breakthroughs in AI, biotechnology, fintech and creative technology. Investment in research, start-up ecosystems and technological ambition is essential. However, the history of the past two decades reveals a troubling pattern: innovation tends to concentrate in already-favoured locations (such as London, Cambridge and Edinburgh) and benefits those already privileged by education, capital and networks. Meanwhile, regions outside the 'golden triangle', older industrial towns, rural areas and communities without prior digital investment find themselves further marginalized. Consequently, the skills gaps widen, broadband access remains patchy and youth unemployment in some regions remains in double digits.

Furthermore, digital sovereignty and the balance between open and closed models will strongly influence whether innovation is widely shared or tightly concentrated: open, sovereign infrastructure can lower barriers for regions and small and medium-sized enterprises (SMEs), while closed, foreign-owned platforms risk deepening dependency and uneven access.

The inclusion challenge is equally urgent. If digital transformation enriches the few while leaving the many behind, it risks eroding social cohesion, fuelling resentment and ultimately undermining the political legitimacy needed for sustained public investment. Citizens who feel excluded from digital opportunities are less likely to trust digital platforms, support digital governance or engage with digital public services. The result is a brittle, fractured digital society where technical innovation advances in elite silos but fails to achieve systemic, societal impact.

The paradox deepens because inclusion is not merely a social good, but an economic necessity. The UK's demographic challenges (led by an ageing population, skills shortages and regional stagnation) cannot be solved by concentrating innovation in one region of the country. True national renewal requires activating talent, potential and innovation across all regions, all communities and all ages. This requires deliberate policy: investment in digital infrastructure outside London, accessible skills development pathways, support for regional tech hubs anchored in local assets (e.g. healthcare in Manchester, creative tech in Bristol, fintech in Edinburgh) and participatory governance that gives communities a voice in shaping how digital technology affects their lives.

The leadership challenge is not to choose between innovation and inclusion, but to embed inclusion as a strategic lever for innovation. This requires recognizing that diverse talent, distributed networks and locally rooted problem-solving will produce richer, more resilient and ultimately more valuable innovation than top-down, centralized approaches.

Paradox 2: speed versus safety

The pace of digital change is relentless and shows no signs of slowing down, with new models, platforms and business practices emerging almost daily. Yet public trust in digital systems rests on visible safety, ethical oversight and meaningful accountability. Policies that stress speed can undermine confidence, while excessive caution may stall urgently needed modernization.

The speed imperative is compelling. AI models are advancing faster than regulation can keep up. Competitors and partners such as the US, China and the EU are moving at unprecedented velocity. The UK risks being left behind if it moves too cautiously. Organizations that hesitate to experiment, adopt new tools and transform their operations will find themselves outcompeted. There is legitimate urgency. The window to establish UK leadership in responsible AI, fintech innovation and digital public services is open now, but may not remain open indefinitely.

Yet history offers a warning. Major digital initiatives that prioritized speed over safety have failed spectacularly in the past: the NHS care records system, abandoned after billions spent and years of botched rollouts;[14] the Horizon Post Office scandal,[15] where inadequate testing and accountability mechanisms destroyed lives and trust; opaque algorithmic decision-making in benefits systems that harmed vulnerable populations because safeguards were not in place.[16] Speed without safety breeds not just failures, but catastrophic losses of public trust – losses that take years to rebuild.

Given these experiences, public confidence in digital systems is fragile. Data breaches, surveillance revelations, algorithmic bias and platform manipulation have eroded citizens' trust in recent years. Citizens are increasingly sceptical of claims that technology will solve problems without risks. They worry about their data, algorithmic discrimination, job displacement and the environmental costs of computing. They want to know: who controls this? Who benefits? How will harm be redressed? These are legitimate concerns. Policies that dismiss them in the name of speed risk provoking backlash, resistance and ultimately slower adoption of beneficial technologies.

The paradox is especially acute in public services. A government digital service that moves fast but produces errors, privacy breaches or exclusionary design will face public outcry and political consequences far worse than if it moved more deliberately. Yet a public sector that moves too slowly to modernize will fail citizens, waste resources and cede leadership to private competitors.

The human cost of prioritizing speed over safety in digital projects is not abstract. Universal Credit, examined in chapter 2, offers the starkest illustration: speed without safety produced years of hardship that undermined the very reforms it was meant to deliver.

Hence, the leadership challenge is not to choose between speed and safety, but to integrate safety into speed by embedding continuous testing, transparent governance, robust audit mechanisms and meaningful accountability into rapid iteration cycles. As discussed later, this is possible: Singapore, Estonia and other digital nations have demonstrated that high-speed innovation and strong safeguards can coexist. The key is treating safety not as an afterthought or compliance burden, but as a competitive advantage that builds trust and enables faster, deeper adoption.

Paradox 3: centralization versus local adaptation

National strategy sets priorities and invests resources, but real change happens locally where public agencies, businesses, and community groups interpret, adapt and apply new technologies to their own realities. The tension is how to balance centralized ambition with support for local context, grassroots problem-solving and community agency.

The centralization argument is strong. National strategies for AI, digital government and skills development provide coherence, prevent wasteful duplication and enable economies of scale. A shared technology stack, national data standards and coordinated investment make sense. Without central direction, regions fragment into incompatible silos, each building their own systems, unable to share data or learn from peers. The UK's historical experience with regional digital initiatives shows that without national coordination local efforts often fail to scale or achieve system-wide impact.[17]

Yet the history of top-down digital transformation is littered with failures. National programs imposed without local input, without understanding regional contexts or without empowering front line practitioners frequently underdeliver. Why? Because digital transformation is not primarily a technical challenge; it is an organizational and cultural issue. Real change requires buy-in from front line staff, understanding of local workflows, adaptation to local needs and iterative learning from what works in practice. These dynamics cannot be mandated from the centre; they emerge from locally rooted collaboration.

The most successful digital transformations in the UK have been those where national strategy set direction but also empowered local implementation. The Government Digital Service (GDS) (described in chapter 2) succeeded precisely because it set principles such as user-centred design, agile delivery, and open standards and let local teams adapt them, rather than dictating implementation. Similarly, NHS trusts that invested in local digital leadership and participatory design succeeded in adoption; those that received mandates from above faced resistance and slower adoption.[18]

The regional diversity of the UK compounds this paradox. Manchester's health innovation ecosystem, for example, is fundamentally different from Edinburgh's fintech cluster, which differs from rural Norfolk's agriculture sector. A 'one-size-fits-all' national AI strategy will fail to activate the unique assets and opportunities of each region. Yet without national coordination, regions cannot pool resources, share learning or achieve scale.

The leadership challenge, therefore, is not to choose between centralization and local adaptation, but to create 'distributed coordination' where national strategy sets direction and resources, but where local implementation is empowered, flexible and participatory. This requires investing in regional leadership capacity, creating feedback loops between central and local actors, supporting peer-to-peer learning across regions, and being willing to adapt national strategy based on local learning. It also requires recognizing that 'local' does not mean isolated; it means nested within national frameworks, drawing on national resources, but adapted to the local context and driven by local agency.

Paradox 4: high-tech leadership versus human relationships

Digital innovation often prioritizes technical prowess, digital platforms and automated efficiency. Yet past waves of transformation show that sustainable progress relies on human relationships with the ability to foster collaboration, trust and adaptable teams. No algorithm can replace the value of skilled, reflexive leadership.

The technology leadership argument is seductive. AI promises to automate routine decisions, optimize processes and free humans from tedious work. Algorithms can process data faster than humans, detect patterns invisible to human cognition and operate at scale. The promise is efficiency, precision and liberation from drudgery. In many domains, such as financial trading, medical imaging, routing optimization or manufacturing quality control, AI delivers real value by automating tasks that are complex, repetitive and time critical. This makes them highly amenable to automation.

However, the evidence from organizational change research is clear: technical capability alone does not drive transformation.[19] Organizations with world-class technology but weak leadership, poor teamwork and low trust fail to adopt and scale that technology effectively. Conversely, organizations with average technology but strong leadership, collaborative culture and investment in people achieve remarkable results.

Why? Because digital transformation is not primarily about technology. It is about changing how people work, how organizations make decisions and how institutions relate to their users. These changes are fundamentally social and relational. They demand trust between front line staff and leadership, ensuring teams have psychological safety to experiment, fail and learn. Furthermore, they require leaders who can communicate vision, address anxiety, support those affected by change and listen to front line learning. This drives investment in coaching, mentoring and collaborative problem-solving. No algorithm can do this work.

Moreover, the most critical decisions in digital transformation – what problems to solve, which values to embed and how to weigh competing interests – are not technical. They are ethical and political, requiring human judgement, democratic deliberation and reflection on what kind of society we want to create. Over-automating these decisions and relying on algorithms without human oversight, public participation and accountability risks losing legitimacy and making decisions that serve narrow interests at the expense of the public good.

The paradox is especially acute in public sector transformation. For example, a health system that optimizes for algorithmic efficiency but loses sight of human care will fail patients and erode trust. Equally, a government system that automates decision-making without transparency or appeal mechanisms will face backlash and legal challenges. Likewise, a school system that relies on algorithmic assessment without human teacher judgement will produce narrow, brittle learning outcomes.

Hence, the leadership challenge is not to choose between technical and human excellence, but to integrate them by investing in high-quality technology while simultaneously investing in leadership development, team building and participatory governance. The best digital leaders are those who combine technical literacy with emotional intelligence, systems thinking with empathy for how change affects people, and ambition for innovation with humility about what technology can and cannot do.

Paradox 5: long-term vision versus short-term results

Public and organizational patience is short: leaders are pressured to deliver 'quick wins', even when everyone agrees that effective transformation depends on sustained investment, learning and iterative progress. The challenge is to deliver visible change now while keeping the focus on the deep, systemic reforms that truly alter how the UK creates and shares value through digital technology.

The short-term pressure is relentless. Political cycles typically run on three-to-five-year timescales, while citizens and voters want to see tangible improvements in their lives now, not vague promises of long-term benefit. Similarly, organizational leaders face quarterly earnings reviews and annual performance targets with funding cycles that reward projects with measurable near-term outcomes.

Additionally, there are real reasons for urgency: the cost of delay is substantial. Every year the UK's digital infrastructure risks lagging behind that of its competitors, with the gap widening as time goes on. Every cohort of young people who leave education without digital skills faces career disadvantage. Every region that fails to invest in tech hubs in the next two-to-three years risks permanent competitive loss.

Quick wins are also psychologically important. They demonstrate momentum, build credibility and enable learning. Small successes create energy and momentum for larger efforts. Visible progress builds public confidence and political support for sustained investment. A leader who delivers nothing for several years will lose support, regardless of long-term vision. So, the focus on short-term results is not irrational; it is strategically necessary.

Yet sustainable digital transformation is fundamentally long-term work. The most valuable innovations, those that create entirely new value, not just incremental improvement, can take many years from initial research investment to societal impact. The shift to agile governance, to participatory culture and to systems thinking requires sustained work that produces benefits gradually, not in discrete quarterly deliverables. Rebuilding regional economies, developing new talent pipelines and embedding new ways of working across large organizations all require sustained effort, measured in years and decades, not quarters and months.

The paradox is particularly acute in digital government and skills. Building trustworthy, inclusive digital public services requires not just technology investment but deep organizational change, culture shift and sustained commitment to participatory governance. These changes cannot be rushed. Even so, pressures for quick wins often push agencies toward near-term lightweight solutions, narrow pilots that do not scale and superficial technology adoption initiatives that leave underlying systems unchanged.

A recurring pattern of bold announcement, promising pilot, failure to scale and project restart has produced cynicism among both practitioners and the public. Chapter 2 analyses this 'pilot trap' in detail. Understanding this is essential because AI adoption risks repeating it.

The leadership challenge is not to choose between short-term wins and long-term vision, but to integrate them through 'strategic patience', delivering visible progress and quick wins that build momentum and credibility while explicitly anchoring those wins within a long-term road map. This requires communicating clearly: 'Here is what we are delivering this year. Here is how it fits into the five-year strategy. Here is the 10-year vision we are building toward'. It requires protecting long-term investments (including research, infrastructure and capability building) from the pressure to deliver short-term results. Then, delivery can be sustained by celebrating milestones and learning from failures, not abandoning strategy when a pilot does not work. Critically, a successful outcome will only be achieved if there is the political courage to sustain investment across electoral cycles and organizational leadership that resists the pressure to declare victory prematurely.

Societal impact and ethical stakes: framing the big questions

Facing up to these paradoxes is critical. With the dramatic advance of digital systems and AI shaping every aspect of our economic, political and social life, we must accept that change is inevitable. Yet this transformation brings more than material change: it demands a fundamental reconsideration of the values and priorities that define society.

We are only just beginning to realize how much is at stake as AI technologies mature and AI adoption becomes widespread. This broad scope and deep disruption raise many important questions for the UK's AI strategy to address.

- *Work and livelihoods.* AI automates tasks once thought uniquely human, altering the landscape of jobs, skills and professional identity. This raises persistent questions: will automation drive mass unemployment, or reinvent work for the better? How can policymakers protect the vulnerable, while enabling opportunity for all?

- *Privacy and autonomy.* Data is 'the new oil' of the digital era,[20] but at what cost? Personal privacy, digital autonomy and the right to meaningful consent are increasingly contested.

What institutional mechanisms are needed to balance innovation with dignity and trust?

- *Power and democracy.* Digital platforms disrupt traditional hierarchies but also concentrate power among new gatekeepers. The design of algorithms and the policies that govern them will shape the future of democracy, free speech and civic participation. Who is accountable for decisions, risks and failures?

- *Equity and justice.* Digital systems can entrench existing inequalities or help overcome them. The choices made in the design, training and deployment of AI systems have profound consequences for discrimination, fairness and inclusion. How can leaders align technology with social justice and opportunity for marginalized groups?

- *Safety and security.* Critical infrastructure, national defence and everyday services now rely on digital and AI systems, thus making failures and attacks ever more costly. What measures can anticipate and prevent catastrophic risks, while preserving openness and dynamism?

Beneath these questions lies a more fundamental one that is rarely asked in government strategy documents: what are the actual cognitive limits of the systems we are building a national strategy around?

It is tempting, as well as being commercially convenient, to describe AI systems as though they 'understand', 'reason' or 'decide'. They do none of these things. As Richard Harper argues,[21] modern AI systems process. That is, they perform extraordinarily sophisticated statistical operations on vast amounts of data. But processing is not thinking. The distinction matters because it determines where AI can be trusted and where it cannot.

LLMs, the technology driving most current AI excitement, work by predicting statistically likely sequences of text. They are, in Erik Larson's words,[22] engines of induction, operating by generalizing from patterns in training data. What they cannot do is abduction: the distinctly human capacity to generate novel hypotheses, make intuitive leaps or exercise judgement in situations where the training data offers no precedent. This is not a temporary limitation awaiting the next model upgrade. It is an architectural feature of how these systems work.

For the leaders reading this book, this distinction has immediate practical consequences. AI systems are powerful tools for tasks where the goal is to apply known patterns consistently (such as screening medical images, detecting financial fraud or processing routine planning applications). They are unreliable tools for tasks where the goal is to exercise judgement about novel situations (such as assessing whether a family is at urgent risk, deciding whether a planning application raises unprecedented environmental concerns, or evaluating whether a scientific result is a breakthrough or a statistical artefact). Any national strategy that does not make this distinction between the domains where AI augments human judgement and the domains where it substitutes for it risks deploying the wrong capability to the highest-stakes decisions.

Leadership imperative: mindsets and practice for a transitional age

As the UK navigates through this digital watershed, a new model of leadership is required, one that goes beyond technical expertise or traditional management prowess. The leaders of today and tomorrow must cultivate a unique blend of strategic vision, adaptive practice and ethical resolve.

In practice, this means that a new mindset for AI adoption is required by digital leaders.

- *Curiosity and continuous learning.* The velocity of change in digital and AI technologies demands leaders who embrace lifelong learning, seek out diverse perspectives and adapt their strategies as new information and capabilities emerge.
- *Humility and collaborative spirit.* No single individual or team can fully understand the opportunities and risks at hand. The most successful leaders listen more than they speak, foster high-trust partnerships and empower others to contribute openly.
- *Risk-taking and resilience.* Transformative innovation requires courage exemplified in a willingness to experiment, accept failure and recover quickly. Leaders must create cultures where 'safe to fail' is not just a slogan, but a lived practice.
- *Systems thinking.* Effective leaders recognize that every policy decision, technology deployment and organizational change ripples through complex networks. Systems thinkers anticipate unintended consequences and focus on sustainable, long-term impact over short-term wins.
- *Ethical stewardship.* Above all, modern leadership demands an unwavering commitment to ethical responsibility. This includes vigilance for bias, dedication to equity and the courage to call out malpractice, even when it is costly or unpopular.
- *Practice in action.* In every industry (including those essential to the UK's future, such as healthcare, finance, education and the creative arts) UK leaders making the most progress are those who pair these mindsets with tangible actions: visible communication, open feedback styles, team mentorship and active engagement with external challenge (from regulators,

activists or competitors). The real force of transformation is found not in bold declarations, but in daily disciplined practice.

Decision-making in the fog: why hedging is rational

These mindsets matter. But they are insufficient without a more honest reckoning with the conditions under which AI decisions are actually made. In practice, leaders do not choose between ‘innovation’ and ‘inclusion’ with full knowledge of the consequences. They make choices in what James March called ‘deeply ambiguous contexts’; situations where the information available is known to be insufficient for the decisions that must be made.[23]

Consider the UK‘s 2025 decision to accept £250 billion in cross-Atlantic AI infrastructure investment. At the time of commitment, neither the implications for digital sovereignty nor the terms of data access were fully knowable. This was not a failure of analysis. It was the nature of the decision itself: a choice made in a specific moment, with specific information, by leaders who knew they were committing resources to a project whose returns and risks would be assessed by their successors.

March called this the ‘rationality of hedging’. Short-term choices are not necessarily short-sighted. When leaders know that today’s information is incomplete, they can rationally choose to preserve future leeway by designing current commitments so that successor decision makers, who will have better information, retain the ability to adjust course. Applied to AI strategy, this means that the goal of a ‘Phase One’ decision is not to get the strategy permanently right, but to keep the maximum number of strategic options open for Phase Two.

This reframing has practical consequences for every leader reading this book. The question to ask of any AI commitment is not only ‘Is this the right decision?’ but ‘Does this decision preserve or close down the options my successor will need?' An AI infrastructure contract that locks the UK into a single hyperscale provider for a decade limits options. A modular, multivendor architecture preserves them. Both may be rational in the short term. Only the second is rational across time.

Conclusions: the watershed moment and the key questions ahead

The UK's journey into a digitally transformed AI future is not a straight line. Rather, it is a zigzagging path populated with moments of collective choice, exposed to contradictions and compromise, and open to endless possibilities. The current watershed moment for AI adoption holds both risk and opportunity, demanding that leaders, practitioners and citizens alike rise to meet the challenges with ambition, humility and determination.

This raises several important questions to explore moving forward.

- How can the UK leverage its historic strengths and contemporary creativity to lead rather than follow in digital transformation?

- What will it take to balance urgency with caution, innovation with inclusion and bold vision with grounded practice?

- How might we develop learning organizations and trusted institutions that can adapt, recover and renew through cycles of technological, economic and societal change?

- How do we build justice and equity into every digital initiative while ensuring that no region, community or person is left behind?

These questions will echo through every chapter of this book and every meeting room, policymaking session and AI strategy workshop in the UK. They will frame the debate for a generation, and their answers will influence not only the trajectory of the digital economy, but the character of our culture and democracy.

As the chapters ahead explore the roots, reforms, sectoral experiences, governance models and ethical imperatives of digital transformation, the goal becomes clear: to create a blueprint for action suited to both the unique demands and enormous promise of the UK's next AI-driven digital era.

CHAPTER 2

Lessons from UK digital transformation

This chapter examines what several decades of UK digital transformation reveal about institutional capability and delivery cultures and why technological ambition repeatedly collides with structural constraints. It provides lessons essential for understanding the current AI opportunities and the challenges ahead.

Introduction: why history matters for AI strategy

The UK's AI strategy is being shaped against the backdrop of decades of digital transformation efforts. Today's challenges of fragmented governance, uneven skills, and persistent gaps between ambition and delivery are not new.[1] Understanding this history is essential because the shortcomings that undermined previous transformation waves persist today.

In its goal to be a leader in AI, the UK possesses important strengths: world-class research institutions, innovative companies, experienced civil servants and deep sectoral expertise. Yet the UK has repeatedly failed to translate these assets into sustained digital transformation. Each digital wave has brought initial promise followed by familiar obstacles: organizational silos, procurement complexity, skills shortages and the difficulty of scaling pilots into systemic change. The question is whether the UK can break these patterns or whether AI transformation will follow the same trajectory.

Patterns of progress and failure: key lessons from four decades

The UK's digital journey has unfolded through recurring cycles: ambitious initiatives launching with political fanfare, implementation encountering stubborn bureaucracy, some projects succeeding through adaptive leadership while others collapse under unrealistic expectations, then a period of recalibration before the next wave begins.

Early digital efforts and the legacy problem

The UK's earliest digital government initiatives emerged in the 1980s and 1990s, driven by faith that technology would streamline bureaucracy and improve service delivery.[2] Large-scale IT projects were commissioned, including a variety of national databases, integrated systems and digital service portals. While some succeeded, many became expensive failures. For example, the NHS National Programme for IT,[3] launched in 2002 with a £12 billion budget, collapsed after spending billions with limited operational benefit. Similarly, the Department of Social Security's IT modernization consumed £2 billion before being abandoned.[4]

In 2004, the National Audit Office report on UK government IT noted that 'the history of such procurements has not been good, with repeated incidences of overspends, delays, performance shortfalls and abandonment at major cost'.[5] The pattern was consistent: underestimated complexity, rigid contracts with major IT vendors, insufficient user engagement and organizational cultures that resisted imposed change.[6]

These failures have contributed to what persists today: legacy systems that are expensive to maintain, difficult to integrate with modern platforms and resistant to replacement. Every subsequent transformation effort must work around or through these inherited constraints. The technical debt accumulated over decades now shapes what is possible with AI adoption.

When technology makes things worse first: the efficiency paradox

There is a deeper pattern in this history that warrants examination, because it will undoubtedly repeat with AI. The introduction of networked computing in UK businesses (and elsewhere) during the 1990s was expected to deliver immediate efficiency gains. What it delivered first was a significant increase in costs. Hardware, training, integration and support expenses rose sharply. Barriers to market entry went up, not down. Far from democratizing competition, early digital infrastructure initially concentrated advantage among those who could afford the investment. The efficiency gains came eventually, but on a timescale and through mechanisms that the original business cases had not anticipated.[7]

The mobile telecommunications story is equally instructive. The business case for Europe's Global System for Mobile Communications (GSM) network was built on corporate efficiency: mobile phones for the mobile workforce. What actually generated transformative value were unforeseen benefits such as the Short Message Service (SMS); a technology that was included in the GSM specification almost as an afterthought, never featured in serious business projections and turned out to matter because it created new forms of social connection that users valued enormously.[8] The commercial breakthrough came not from the efficiency the system was designed to provide, but from a social practice that nobody had planned for. This pattern of infrastructure built for one purpose generating its real value through an entirely different use has profound implications for AI strategy.

Consider the current landscape. UK organizations are investing heavily in LLM-based tools on the assumption that they will improve knowledge-worker productivity. But early evidence suggests a more complex picture. In many deployments, LLMs are functioning less as 'intelligent assistants' and more as expensive substitutes for tasks that traditional search engines already perform adequately.[9] A civil servant who asks an AI chatbot to summarize a policy document is not necessarily more productive than one who reads the executive summary. The compute cost, however, is orders of magnitude greater. If AI adoption cannibalizes existing efficient processes (such as web search and structured document retrieval) without delivering entirely new capabilities, the UK risks a repeat of the 1990s: large upfront costs with delayed and uncertain returns.

The lesson for strategy is not that AI will fail. It is that the path to value is unlikely to follow the projections in current business cases. Leaders who build their strategies around assumed efficiency gains may find themselves, like their 1990s predecessors, managing cost increases and unexpected disruption before any returns materialize. The adaptive response is to plan for this: budget for a period of negative returns, look for the 'SMS equivalent' (the unexpected social or organizational practice that will generate AI's real value) and avoid locking in commitments that assume linear progress.

The GDS revolution and its limits

The creation of the GDS in 2011 gave renewed energy and political visibility to approaches (such as agile development, user-centred design and cross-government platforms) that had been practised in pockets of government for years, but without sustained senior backing or institutional mandate.[10] GDS's contribution was to elevate these methods from niche practice to national standard, backed by ministerial authority and a mandate to challenge departmental inertia. The consolidation of government websites under GOV.UK built on the substantial work of Directgov, which had already brought more than 95% of government services onto a single platform. GDS redesigned the interface, established new design standards and created a brand that became internationally recognized.

GDS also pioneered shared platforms (e.g. GOV.UK Pay, Notify and Verify) that aimed to reduce duplication across government. These built on earlier cross-government components (including payment and alerts systems) that had demonstrated the principle, though often with less visibility and design polish. GDS's design principles, open-source approach and visible advocacy for user needs were influential both domestically and internationally.

Understood in structural terms, GDS pulled two levers simultaneously. On the demand side, it consolidated: one website, common platforms, shared service standards and (critically) spend controls that gave GDS joint authority with the Treasury over departmental IT budgets. On the supply side, it diversified: the Digital Marketplace broke the grip of incumbent systems integrators and opened government contracts to SMEs. This combination of consolidated demand with diversified supply was the institutional mechanism that made GDS's design ambitions achievable rather than aspirational.

Yet GDS also revealed the limitations that AI strategy is likely to come up against.[11] Its early successes came from having political protection, talented teams and freedom to operate outside normal constraints. As it attempted to scale, it encountered the organizational resistance it had initially bypassed. Departments struggled to adopt new methods within existing budget cycles and accountability frameworks. By the late 2010s, much of the early momentum had been absorbed back into more traditional structures.

More fundamentally, GDS's model contained a structural limitation that has become clearer with time. By defining 'services' primarily as user-facing transactions (e.g. forms, applications and information pages) and by developing a Service Standard focused on the user experience of those transactions, GDS created an operational separation between digital delivery and policy design. The Service Standard contains no checkpoints for whether a digital system correctly implements the underlying legislation, administrative law or constitutional requirements it is meant to enact. This separation had consequences. When applied to complex policy programmes, the result was digital systems that were well-designed in interface terms but could fail to implement their own legislation correctly, a shortcoming examined in detail in the Universal Credit analysis that follows.

The lesson for AI strategy is clear. If AI tools are deployed in government using the same separated methodology of optimizing the user-facing layer without integrating the underlying policy logic, the UK may repeat this structural mistake at greater scale and cost.

The Covid-19 pandemic: acceleration and exposure

Another key lesson from this period is that digital transformation does not follow a linear path. The brutal effects of the Covid-19 pandemic acted as both a test of and accelerator for digital transformation. Remote everything (work, health, schooling, social services, etc.) became a necessity overnight. The pandemic forced rapid digital adoption across government, business and society. Services that had resisted digitization for years moved online within weeks. This acceleration exposed both capability and fragility. Organizations with prior digital investment adapted; those without struggled. The digital divide widened as vulnerable populations lacked access to or skills for remote services.[12]

The crisis revealed that the UK possesses substantial capacity for rapid adaptation under extreme pressure. It also demonstrated that such capacity remains unevenly distributed. The same shortcomings apparent before Covid-19 (regional differences, sectoral variation and dependence on individual champions) simply became more obvious and consequential during the crisis.[13]

Delivering digital government at scale

In the aftermath of the pandemic, much of the analysis of the digital successes pointed to a reliance on 'heroic efforts' and temporary workarounds rather than sustainable, systemic change.[14] To address these structural weaknesses, the UK government established the Central Digital and Data Office to provide the strategic leadership and cross-departmental standards that were previously missing. This shift reflects a move away from the isolated delivery of digital 'front ends' toward a more comprehensive digital government at scale strategy aimed at modernizing the underlying technical architecture of the entire state.

However, despite this renewed strategic focus, persistent barriers have continued to hinder long-term progress. A primary obstacle is the vast amount of 'technical debt' tied to legacy systems, which are often decades old, expensive to maintain and difficult to integrate with modern data standards.[15] This is compounded by government funding models that remain poorly suited to digital era governance, often favouring large-scale, one-off capital investments rather than the flexible, iterative funding required for more agile development and delivery styles. Furthermore, a (worsening) critical shortage of high-level digital and data skills within the civil service remains a bottleneck, forcing a continued reliance on external contractors and slowing the cultural shift necessary to embed digital-first thinking into the core of policy design and operational delivery.

Sectoral variation: where transformation succeeds and fails

While common features can be found, in practice the UK's digital economy is a mix of sectoral successes and cautionary tales. Digital transformation outcomes vary dramatically across UK sectors, revealing that success depends less on technology availability than on institutional conditions that enable or prevent change.

Finance and fintech: market-driven success

London's finance sector was an early adopter of automation, global transactions and digital networks.[16] The sector demonstrates what is possible when regulatory innovation, technical capability and market incentives align.[17]

A key example is Open Banking, which was launched in 2018 and which allows major banks to provide API (application programming interface) access to customer data with their consent, enabling third-party services.[18] This regulatory intervention created a platform for innovation that has generated hundreds of new financial services. The combination of regulatory clarity, technical standards and competitive pressure drove authentic transformation. Open Banking demonstrates that regulatory innovation can enable market-driven transformation when government establishes clear standards and enables competition without mandating specific technologies.[19]

However, finance also reveals transformation limits. Algorithmic trading created systemic fragility, as evidenced by flash crashes. AI-driven credit decisions perpetuate historical discrimination. The sector's success at innovation has not translated into addressing embedded inequality or ensuring algorithmic accountability. Speed of adoption does not guarantee responsible implementation.

The pensions sector presents an equally significant, and arguably more complex, test case. With one of the largest concentrations of citizen-held data in the UK, spanning retirees through to the twenty million defined-contribution savers enrolled under auto-enrolment, pensions sit at the intersection of AI capability and institutional readiness. AI is already delivering results in investment trading and has clear potential to personalize individual retirement plans and monitor them at a cost that is accessible to all savers, not just the wealthy. The Pension Schemes Bill 2025 signals that the legislative framework is beginning to catch up with the technology. But as with Open Banking, the determining factor will not be the sophistication of the AI models. Rather, it will be the governance, data-sharing infrastructure and institutional coordination that determine whether these capabilities reach the people who need them.

Healthcare: ambition constrained by complexity

The NHS represents one of the biggest challenges for transformation: massive scale, legacy IT infrastructure, fragmented governance across trusts and regions, workforce skills gaps and life-or-death consequences of failure. Digital health initiatives have achieved pockets of excellence in specific trusts with effective electronic records, successful telemedicine pilots and AI diagnostic tools in particular specialties.[20] But systemic transformation remains elusive.

The barriers are instructive:[21]

- procurement processes designed for physical equipment struggle with iterative software development;
- clinical staff lack time and training for new systems;
- governance fragmentation means that a successful pilot in one trust cannot easily be transferred to another;
- patient data remains siloed across incompatible systems.

These are not technical problems but institutional ones, and they are shared by all large, complex, safety-critical institutions attempting transformation.

Creative industries and SMEs: innovation without support

The UK's creative and technology sectors demonstrate entrepreneurial capability, generating globally competitive companies and innovative digital services.[22] Yet scale-up remains difficult. Several successful UK start-ups have relocated or been acquired by foreign companies because the UK lacks the venture funding, talent pools and growth infrastructure available in the US or, increasingly, Europe. SMEs across sectors struggle with digital adoption due to cost, complexity and the absence of tailored support.[23] The UK excels at generating innovation but struggles to translate it into sustained domestic capability.

Manufacturing and infrastructure
In manufacturing and supply chain logistics, the UK's digital adoption is uneven. Advanced robotics, digital twins and materials science labs in innovative clusters (e.g. the Midlands, the North East) contrast with slower rollouts elsewhere. Legacy industrial infrastructure, patchy broadband and workforce inertia slow the spread of digital innovation, causing concern that the UK is falling behind global leaders in robotics and AI.[24]

Start-ups and entrepreneurial ecosystems
Venture capital, accelerators and entrepreneurial universities form a thriving start-up ecosystem, with particular success in fintech, healthtech, advanced image processing and cleantech. UK tech entrepreneurship benefits from a dense, collaborative network, supportive policy interventions (e.g. R&D tax credits) and international mobility.[25] But scale-up gaps and access inequities persist, especially outside London and South East England.[26]

Recurring barriers: why transformation stalls

The case studies and high-level reviews presented above offer interesting glimpses into the opportunities and challenges of digital transformation. Across sectors and decades, similar obstacles repeatedly prevent transformation from achieving stated ambitions. Understanding these failures is essential because they will constrain AI adoption unless deliberately addressed.

Legacy IT and infrastructure drag

Decades of accumulated technical debt, bespoke systems and outdated architecture mean that public organizations often spend more maintaining the past than investing in the future. A recent UK government review noted that organizations such as the Department for Work and Pensions (DWP) and NHS England spend as much as 75%–80% of their technology budgets on upkeep rather than on modernization.[27] Large-scale transformation often depends on integrating or replacing legacy platforms, a process fraught with risk, disruption and massive cost overruns.

Governance fragmentation

UK digital transformation operates within fragmented governance: different departments pursuing different priorities, national government strategies colliding with local implementation realities and sectoral regulators interpreting policies differently. This fragmentation means that coherent transformation requires coordination across organizational boundaries, where natural incentives or mechanisms for alignment are often lacking. National strategies that announce bold initiatives are useful. However, change depends on hundreds of organizations making compatible choices. Without coordination mechanisms, initiatives remain disconnected and transformation remains sporadic rather than systemic.

Procurement as barrier

Traditional public sector procurement frameworks were designed for physical infrastructure and standardized services.

They require detailed upfront specifications, fixed-price contracts and risk transfer to suppliers. These assumptions are largely incompatible with agile forms of digital delivery, which depend on iteration, learning and adaptive change. Attempts at more flexible digital service procurement such as G-Cloud have helped.[28] However, procurement remains a barrier that prevents the adaptive approaches that successful digital transformation requires. Reform has been repeatedly attempted and repeatedly stalled due to a combination of audit concerns, risk aversion and resistance from established contractors.[29]

Skills gaps and talent retention

Digital skills shortages affect every sector but have distinct impacts in different contexts. The UK government struggles to recruit and retain technical talent due to civil service pay scales that cannot compete with private sector alternatives. The 2025 UK State of Digital Government Review concluded that up to 50% of digital and data roles across the government remained unfilled or were being filled by expensive external contractors.

Meanwhile, in areas such as the NHS, the need for staff who understand both the domain and digital systems makes recruitment even harder. Additionally, small businesses lack resources for training or specialist hiring. These are not temporary recruitment challenges but structural misalignments between what transformation requires and what current systems can provide. Without sustained investment in skills development across educational levels and career stages, capability gaps will constrain AI adoption regardless of technological progress.

The pilot trap

UK transformation efforts generate impressive pilots: controlled experiments demonstrating what new digitally-driven approaches can achieve. Pilots succeed because they receive dedicated resources, political protection and freedom from normal constraints. The problem is scaling. Organizations struggle when moving from protected demonstration to routine operation across organizations facing budget pressure, accountability requirements and operational complexity. Most pilots never scale.[30] Instead, organizations move to the next pilot, accumulating demonstration successes that do not translate into systemic capability. This pattern has persisted for decades. Breaking it requires different approaches to both pilots and scaling, treating them as distinct challenges requiring distinct capabilities.

Reality check: the pilot trap is a choice, not fate

The UK's pattern of impressive pilots that never scale is not inevitable. Rather, it is the result of specific structural choices.

Pilots succeed because they receive dedicated resources, political protection and freedom from normal constraints. Talented teams get autonomy to experiment. Budget pressures are suspended. Accountability frameworks are relaxed. Governance requirements are waived. The pilot operates in a protected bubble where innovation can flourish precisely because it is isolated from the organizational immune system that would normally reject it.

The question is not 'why don't pilots scale?'. It is 'are we willing to extend pilot conditions to broader implementation?'. Scaling means accepting that business-as-usual (BAU) teams will implement with less expertise, tighter budgets and more constraints than pilot teams enjoyed. It means tolerating initially lower performance as organizations learn. It means protecting scaled initiatives from the same governance friction, risk aversion and resource competition that pilots bypassed.

This is why scaling rarely happens. Organizations learn from pilots, declare success, then expect BAU teams to replicate results without replicating conditions. When performance disappoints, the response is to commission another pilot with another talented team in another protected space. The cycle repeats.

Breaking this pattern requires uncomfortable choices. Either institutionalize the conditions that enable pilots – which means fundamentally restructuring how organizations operate – or accept that transformation will continue to be through episodic demonstrations rather than systemic change. The UK has chosen the former for two decades while describing it as the latter. The question is whether leaders have the institutional courage to make a different choice or whether the pilot trap reflects legitimate constraints that rhetoric cannot overcome.

What enables success: conditions for lasting change

Amid the failures and stalled transformations, some initiatives have achieved lasting change. Understanding what enabled these successes reveals what systemic transformation will require.

First, clear regulatory frameworks coupled with market incentives have proven to be effective where both exist, as demonstrated by Open Banking and certain fintech innovations. However, this model only works in contexts where market mechanisms are appropriate and where regulation is sophisticated enough to anticipate, rather than react to, change.

Second, sustained political commitment that survives churn such as short electoral cycles has been essential for long-term transformation. For instance, the rare initiatives that maintained funding and focus across changes of government succeeded while more ambitious efforts without cross-party support were abandoned when attention shifted. This suggests that transformation requires depoliticizing core digital infrastructure decisions and treating them like physical infrastructure that continues regardless of who is in charge.

Third, user-centred design approaches that have involved the affected populations in development have consistently performed better than top-down mandates. Solutions such as the NHS App, the essential 'digital front door' to the UK health service, which has more than 40 million downloads, offer a 'person-centric' service that meets the expectations of the digital age.[31] This requires organizational cultures that value learning and iteration over certainty and control. Where such cultures exist (often in small teams or protected spaces), transformation succeeds. Where they do not, technical capability alone proves insufficient.

Finally, cross-functional teams combining technical, domain and delivery expertise have outperformed siloed specialists. GDS demonstrated this; successful digital health initiatives replicated it; innovative local councils have built on it. But creating such teams requires HR systems that enable talent mobility, leadership that protects cross-boundary collaboration and metrics that reward collective success over individual performance. Most organizations lack these conditions.

Implications for AI transformation

The lessons from four decades of digital transformation suggest that the UK's AI ambitions will face familiar obstacles unless institutional conditions change.

Current AI strategy assumes that providing access to technology, funding research and establishing principles will drive adoption. History suggests otherwise. The barriers to transformation are not primarily technical or financial but institutional: governance fragmentation that prevents coordination, procurement systems that block adaptive approaches, skills gaps that limit implementation capacity and organizational cultures that resist change.

AI adoption is already following the pattern of previous waves:[32] impressive pilots demonstrating potential, uneven sectoral progress with finance and technology moving fastest while public services and SMEs lag, initial enthusiasm followed by a growing awareness of implementation complexity, and a gradual realization that transformation requires institutional change not just access to technology.[33]

Breaking this pattern requires more than technical fixes; it demands the political courage to confront deep-seated structural barriers. The following chapters examine whether the UK can finally move beyond a history of isolated pilots and unscaled innovation, leveraging the current sense of urgency to achieve true systemic transformation.

Conclusions: lessons from digital transformation

Digital transformation in the UK has repeatedly demonstrated that technical capability alone does not drive institutional change; success requires aligned governance, appropriate procurement, sustained skills investment and organizational cultures that enable adaptation. The pattern of impressive pilots failing to scale has persisted across decades and sectors, revealing that demonstration and implementation require fundamentally different capabilities and conditions.

GDS proved that user-centred, agile approaches can succeed in government but also demonstrated the difficulty of sustaining such approaches when they conflict with established accountability frameworks and organizational structures. Major failures as experienced with NHS IT overspends, school exam algorithm errors and the delayed Universal Credit rollout share common characteristics: underestimated complexity, insufficient user engagement, rigid contracts and organizational resistance; these patterns will constrain AI adoption unless deliberately addressed.

Universal Credit illustrates these patterns at their most consequential.[34] Speed without preparation certainly played a role: the programme spent £425 million and had no users by its original

2013 deadline. But the deeper failure was structural, not operational. Universal Credit was designed using a methodology that treated the digital system as a 'service' to be optimized for users – a task handed to digital teams operating under a standard that measured user experience but included no checks for whether the system correctly implemented its enabling legislation.

The result was a digital service that looked modern and was, in narrow interface terms, well designed, but that routinely breached rule-of-law principles. Its decision-making processes were opaque to the citizens they affected. Its automation embedded errors that, for benefit claimants, translated into hunger, debt and lost housing. The 'reset' that eventually occurred addressed some operational failures but did not resolve the underlying design separation. The lesson extends beyond benefits administration: when digital systems that enact legislation are designed by teams whose standard does not require them to verify legislative compliance, the failure is not accidental but structural.

The design gap: when service design is separate from policy design

A deeper lesson runs beneath these individual failures, one that has particular urgency for AI strategy. The dominant approach to digital government over the past decade has been to treat 'service design' as primarily a question of user interface and transaction design (how a citizen interacts with a screen, fills in a form or receives a notification). This approach produced measurable improvements in usability and accessibility. But it also created an operational separation between the teams designing the digital interface and the teams responsible for the policy, legislation and administrative law that the interface is meant to implement.

The consequences of this separation have been significant. For example, when a digital system processes benefit claims, it is not merely providing a user experience, it is enacting legislation. When it triages court cases or allocates school places, it is making decisions that must comply with statutory requirements and constitutional principles. If the team designing the digital system operates to a standard that assesses user experience but includes no safeguards for legislative compliance, the result can be a service that is well-designed in interface terms but fails to implement its own legal mandate. This is not a hypothetical risk. It is what happened with Universal Credit, where the digital system's design decisions breached rule-of-law principles, not because the technology failed, but because the design process treated policy implementation as someone else's responsibility.

For AI strategy, the lesson is clear. Generative AI tools deployed on unreformed processes will inherit whatever dysfunction underlies them. The result is what this book terms a 'digital veneer': a new layer of technology that creates the appearance of modernization while fossilizing unreformed structures. This is a topic explored further in chapter 3.

The implication is that AI deployment in government (and in any complex institutional setting) cannot proceed independently of a review of the underlying policy, legislation, data and processes. Technology design and policy design must be integrated from the start, not treated as separate workstreams operating to separate standards. This is one of the most consequential lesson of the UK's digital transformation experience, and the one most at risk of being repeated if AI adoption follows the same institutional patterns.

Successful transformations such as Open Banking, certain fintech innovations and several digital health initiatives have combined regulatory clarity, market incentives, sustained political commitment and cross-functional teams. However, replicating these conditions more broadly requires institutional reforms that current structures resist, and a series of targeted strategic initiatives, which are outlined in the subsequent chapters.

PART II

WHAT MATTERS NOW

CHAPTER 3

The UK's AI challenge and opportunity today

The patterns identified in the previous chapter – governance fragmentation, procurement barriers and the pilot trap – are not merely historical. They are active constraints shaping the UK's AI ambitions today. This chapter examines the gap between the UK's stated AI strategy and what is actually happening across sectors.

It does this systematically by mapping the UK's AI ambitions as expressed in national strategies and sector initiatives; considering what happens when those ambitions meet operational reality across finance, health, creative industries and infrastructure; exploring the leadership stories that illuminate both possibilities and pitfalls; diagnosing the systemic barriers that repeatedly prevent transformation from taking root; and establishing where intervention could create real leverage. The analysis moves from the particular to the systemic, from individual cases to recurring patterns, ultimately confronting a central question: can UK institutions become truly adaptive, or will structural inertia condemn the country to perpetual cycles of ambitious launch and disappointing delivery?

The stakes extend beyond economic competitiveness. How the UK navigates AI transformation will determine whether algorithmic systems strengthen democratic accountability or undermine it, whether digital infrastructure enhances national resilience or creates new dependencies and whether technological change reduces societal inequalities or amplifies them. Understanding why ambition repeatedly falls short of implementation is the necessary foundation for designing institutions capable of delivering on the UK's AI potential.

Introduction: the ambition–reality gap

In mapping the scale of the UK's AI opportunity, chapter 1 also disclosed the tension between that ambition and questions of digital sovereignty, exploring whether the UK is securing capability or renting access. This chapter examines a different but related gap: between what UK leaders declare they will accomplish and what institutions actually deliver.

This is not a new problem. Understanding why this gap persists, and what would be required to close it, is essential groundwork for the institutional reforms that follow.

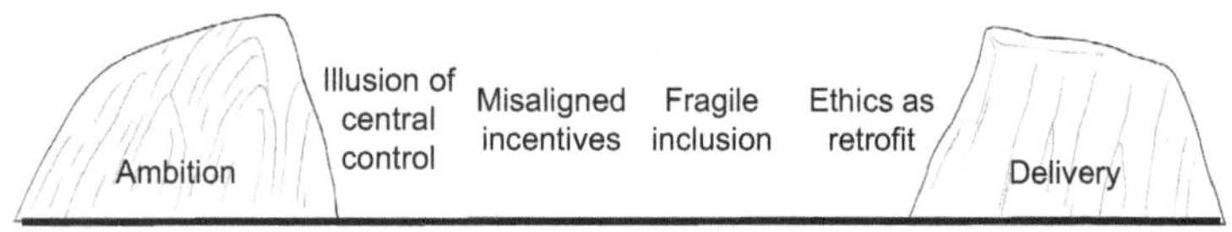

Figure 2. Bridging the gap between ambition and delivery

The stories of ambition and implementation in this chapter are not isolated narratives. They are expressions of deeper, systemic patterns that repeat across sectors, regions and decades. When a digital government initiative falters, it is rarely because the technology was wrong or the people uncommitted. More often, failure reflects misalignment between what an innovative team can achieve in a protected space and what the broader system will support, sustain or scale. When an AI pilot succeeds but fails to spread, the bottleneck is typically not technical capability but organizational culture, policy architecture or the absence of incentive structures that reward adaptation.

To understand these patterns is to recognize that transformation in the UK's digital and AI future depends less on singular breakthroughs than on systemic reform: facing up to how institutions are structured, how power is distributed, how incentives align or clash and how learning is embedded or ignored.

Reality check: precision, discovery and the consensus trap

Before mapping the UK's AI ambitions across sectors, we must confront a foundational assumption that runs through most government strategy documents: that 'AI' is a single technology requiring a single strategy. It is not.

Consider two institutions that will feature prominently in the UK's AI future: the NHS and the Francis Crick Institute. Both will use tools built on transformer architectures and LLMs. But they are using them for fundamentally different purposes, and confusing those purposes is a strategic error.

In NHS administration, AI's value lies in precision and equivalence: ensuring that a patient in Newcastle receives the same quality of triage as one in London, that diagnostic imaging is read consistently and that resource allocation follows evidence rather than accident. Here, the tendency of deep learning systems to converge on statistical averages is a feature. Consistency is the goal.

In scientific research, the goal is the opposite: discovery. Breakthroughs happen at the margins; in outlier results and unexpected patterns that statistical averaging would smooth away. A drug discovery AI system that converges on the consensus of existing research may be efficient, but it is unlikely to find the novel compound that existing knowledge does not predict. As Gary Marcus and Ernest Davis observed in their book *Rebooting AI*, AI systems built on pattern-matching in large organizations are structurally biased toward reproducing what is already known. This is the 'consensus trap': the deeper the training data, the stronger the pull toward the average. This is precisely the opposite of what frontier science requires.

The strategic implication is that a single 'national AI strategy' that does not distinguish between these modes risks applying the wrong tool to the wrong problem. AI procurement for the NHS should prioritize consistency, audit trails and explainability. AI procurement for UK Research and Innovation should prioritize flexibility, human-in-the-loop override and tolerance for surprising outputs. These are different capabilities, different risk profiles and different governance requirements. They should be treated as such.

Mapping the UK's AI ambitions

The last decade has been defined by the proliferation of UK national AI road maps, sector deals, white papers and summit declarations. These are not merely technical documents, but blueprints for a new digital era, providing rallying calls to industry, research and government to act in concert.

The UK national AI strategy

The most comprehensive statement on the UK's AI ambitions can be seen in the UK's National AI Strategy.[1] Released in 2021 (and subsequently updated), it positions AI as the focal point for productivity, inclusivity and global competitiveness. The document anchors ambition in three pillars: boosting the UK's AI ecosystem, fostering responsible innovation and leveraging AI for public benefit. Its vision is expansive, describing the UK as an AI superpower that is 'well placed to lead the world over the next decade as a genuine research and innovation powerhouse, a hive of global talent and a progressive regulatory and business environment'.

Sector deals establishing agreements between the government and key industries have translated this high-level ambition into more grounded commitments. Investments in health, creative industries and energy have combined funding for talent, regulatory reform and cross-sector partnership. The published road map has brought alignment around strategic priorities such as digital skills, trusted regulatory frameworks, ethical standards and a 'whole-of-government' approach to adoption.

Policy proliferation: opportunities and risks

While ambition has triggered significant investment and mobilization, it has also produced risks. Policy cycles are faster than delivery cycles. Announcements outpace implementation and the number of new strategies often overwhelms the capacity for legitimate reform. Critics argue that national ambition risks devolving into 'pilot fatigue', where programs are launched and relaunched, yet fail to scale into durable institutional change.[2]

The creation of new agencies (such as the Office for AI and the Centre for Data Ethics and Innovation), national grand challenges and summit events have helped the UK define an AI leadership position. However, the translation from strategy to delivery depends on sectoral coordination, regional engagement and sustained commitment across businesses, researchers, policy makers and civil society.

From rhetoric to results

While technology provides the tools for change, it is human initiative and action that determine the rate of adoption. Bridging the gap between high-level ambition and tangible delivery requires deep institutional trust. Belief must be strong among front line professionals that new systems will enhance, rather than hinder, their ability to serve clients. Without this foundation, even the most sophisticated strategies encounter substantial scepticism, often manifesting as passive resistance. Therefore, the primary challenge of modernization is not just an engineering task, but a social one: proving that the digital future is both dependable and designed with the practitioner in mind.

Such trust is built not through white papers, but on the ground when clinicians, teachers, analysts, social workers and entrepreneurs work together to turn opportunity into impact. The UK's ambition must reckon with deep-rooted operational realities: legacy IT in government and health, fragmented data infrastructure, the slow pace of regulatory change and intense competition for talent. Without demonstrable results that improve front line practice, even the most sophisticated strategies will encounter scepticism and passive resistance.

Digital identity: a foundational test case

An interesting example of where these issues surface is in the UK's approach to digital identity,[3] a fundamental concept for delivering digital services. The 2025 announcement of a new digital identity programme represents more than a policy shift; it is a high-stakes test of public confidence. While it is a strategic recognition that effective AI deployment across public services and business operations demands reliable, interoperable identity infrastructure, its ultimate success hinges on a central question: will the public trust the UK government with their most sensitive personal data?

This is not simply about replacing physical cards with digital ones. It is about creating the foundational layer on which more intelligent, responsive systems of governance and commerce can be built. However, that foundation is only as strong as the public's belief that the government can deliver on its promises of secure privacy and robust security. Without reliable identity infrastructure, and the deep-seated trust that must underpin it, AI systems cannot safely verify users, personalize services or maintain the social license necessary for widespread adoption.

The current challenge is acute. The UK's inability to reliably identify citizens and accurately match them to services undermines effective public service delivery. This fragmentation creates inefficiencies through repeated authentication, fraud vulnerabilities and barriers to coordinated care. To overcome this, the government must move beyond technical fixes and address the underlying concern of whether it can be a reliable steward of the digital citizen. The true criterion of success for this programme will not just be technical interoperability, but the establishment of a durable bond of trust between the state and the individual regarding data privacy.

The stakes are high, and the UK's track record is mixed. Digital identity will succeed only if it avoids the structural pitfalls identified in chapter 2, particularly the separation of service design from policy implementation that undermined Universal Credit.

Sector realities: where ambition meets implementation

The barriers to AI adoption are not uniform across the economy. They are deeply rooted in the unique operational cultures and regulatory landscapes of individual industries. A fintech start-up may find the primary hurdle to be market competition, while a hospital must navigate complex ethical safeguards, sensitive data privacy requirements and the rigidities of public sector procurement. Understanding these variations reveals why solutions that thrive in one environment may stall in another.

What emerges across UK sectors is a picture of uneven progress, with pockets of clear innovation existing alongside persistent barriers, promising pilots that struggle to scale, and leadership efforts that generate real change in some contexts while being absorbed and neutralized by system constraints in others.

Finance and fintech

The UK's fintech sector is globally renowned, home to institutions such as Monzo, Revolut and Starling, as well as innovation platforms such as Open Banking. Machine learning powers credit risk modelling, anti-fraud algorithms and personalized customer experience. The UK's regulatory approach based on balancing competitive innovation with systemic stability has drawn international attention.

Yet this leadership is fragile. Digital exclusion persists in rural and disadvantaged communities. Legacy banking infrastructure slows progress. Talent retention is threatened by global competition. The defining challenge in this sector is trust. Cybersecurity, algorithmic transparency and ethical AI set the parameters for legitimacy and market resilience. Recent high-profile breaches and regulatory investigations around consumer data, algorithmic bias and responsible lending have prompted recalibration of risk management, governance and consumer protection.

Health and life sciences

The NHS has been described as AI's most promising frontier.[4] Diagnostic support, personalized medicine, drug discovery, and operational optimization all offer the tantalizing promise of healthcare renewal at a time of growing backlogs and increasing delivery costs. Initiatives such as the NHS AI Lab, partnerships with DeepMind, and national imaging collaborations have shown initial success in the fields of radiology, pathology, and genomics.

Scaling success is far harder. NHS trusts vary enormously in terms of digital maturity. Legacy electronic health records, siloed data systems and concerns around commercial access to patient data pose formidable barriers. Clinicians worry about automation bias, liability and the deskilling of medical judgement. The public demands assurance that AI will augment, not replace, the human connection at the heart of care.

Governance remains complex and contested. The boundary between research, service improvement and commercial exploitation is thin. Questions around consent, data linkage and the use of synthetic datasets persist. Ethical oversight is necessary but sometimes slows urgently needed innovation. The sector illustrates how technical promise collides with operational legacy, trust deficits and the tension between innovation and accountability.

Creative industries

The UK creative sector (including film, music, gaming, advertising and fashion industries) has embraced AI-driven tools for generative design, audience analytics, content personalization and production efficiency. Independent studios, global platforms and universities collaborate in testing algorithmic art and virtual worlds.

However, creative workers are simultaneously excited and alarmed. Generative AI raises urgent intellectual property and attribution questions: who owns algorithmically generated content? How are artists compensated when algorithms are trained on their work? Will algorithmic curation favour mainstream tastes, eroding creative diversity?

The sector is also characterized by stark inequalities. London-based platforms and well-funded studios enjoy privileged access to talent and infrastructure, while regional artists struggle for investment and recognition. AI systems built on narrow datasets risk reinforcing cultural stereotypes and marginalizing voices outside dominant narratives. For the creative sector, digital sovereignty plays out as the question of who controls cultural production.

Infrastructure, energy and net zero

Energy and critical infrastructure present some of the UK's most urgent AI applications: smart grids, demand forecasting, renewable energy integration and predictive maintenance. These sectors face immense pressure to decarbonize, modernize aging infrastructure and meet net zero commitments.

Pilot projects abound in areas such as AI-driven energy optimization in buildings, algorithmic trading in renewable energy markets, predictive analytics for transport infrastructure. Partnerships between utilities, local authorities and tech firms demonstrate real innovation.

However, integration and scaling of these AI-driven advances remains patchy. The UK's energy and transport networks are among the world's oldest, and retrofitting digital systems to Victorian-era infrastructure is slow, expensive and risky. Furthermore, governance is fragmented, with a patchwork of regional authorities, national regulators and commercial providers operating in separate policy silos. Capital allocation remains a bottleneck, with public funding skewed toward high-profile projects and legacy asset owners reluctant to invest without guaranteed returns.

For energy and infrastructure, transparency and distributed ownership are critical for resilience. Digital sovereignty concerns mean that if grid management algorithms are proprietary black boxes controlled by foreign vendors, the UK's ability to respond to energy crises or system failures is constrained.

The pattern across sectors

Implementation is where ambition meets reality. The UK's aspirations for AI leadership are distinguished by sectoral variation consisting of locally adapted efforts marked by trial, error, learning and renegotiation. But the recurring pattern is clear. Promising pilots struggle to become standard practice, and pockets of excellence remain isolated rather than spreading across systems.

Reality check: scale-up or lock-in?

The emphasis on 'scaling innovation' from successful pilots obscures a more fundamental question: are we scaling the right things?

The UK has become expert at creating innovation sandboxes, accelerator programs and pilot projects. These generate impressive demonstrations and positive case studies. But pilot success and systemic transformation are different challenges requiring different capabilities. A healthcare AI that works brilliantly in a single well-resourced trust with enthusiastic clinical champions may fail completely when deployed across the NHS's complex landscape of legacy systems, varied capabilities and constrained resources.

The current approach risks creating what might be called 'demonstration-ware', with impressive showcases that never achieve the boring, unglamorous work of operating reliably at scale under real-world constraints. Worse, the pressure to show innovation success creates incentives to declare pilots successful prematurely, to scale before foundations are solid and to move to the next demonstration before learning from the last one. The UK needs fewer pilots and more systematic capability building in the institutions that must sustain transformation after the innovation teams have moved on.

Leadership: success, failure and what they teach us

The success of the UK's AI ambitions will be shaped as much by leadership and values-driven choices as by policy and technology. Examining specific cases, whether triumphs or failures, reveals what effective leadership demands.

Open Banking: regulatory courage

Open Banking stands as perhaps the UK's clearest AI-adjacent success story.[5] UK policymakers and fintech leaders championed regulatory reform that enabled data portability and consumer choice, making the UK a global model for competitive innovation. The initiative succeeded because it combined regulatory mandate with industry collaboration, set clear technical standards while allowing market experimentation and maintained sustained political commitment through implementation challenges. Leaders built coalitions across traditional banking, fintech start-ups, consumer advocates and regulators, demonstrating that transformation requires bridging institutional boundaries, not just technical excellence.

NHS data partnerships: trust betrayed

Several NHS data-sharing agreements with commercial AI firms faced public backlash over consent, transparency and governance, forcing renegotiation. The 2017 Royal Free/DeepMind episode,[6] where patient data was shared without explicit consent, sparked national debate and led to strengthened ethics frameworks. Such cases illustrate how even well-intentioned leaders can lose public trust when process and inclusion are sidelined. Technical capability became secondary once citizens questioned whether their interests were being protected.

The 2020 exam algorithm: speed without safeguards

The 2020 exam algorithm crisis, examined in chapter 6, demonstrated how algorithmic opacity combined with inappropriate haste could shatter public trust overnight.

What these cases reveal

Effective leaders in AI transformation share common characteristics. They combine optimism with critical scepticism. They build coalitions across professional and institutional boundaries. They prioritize trust-building as much as technical deployment. And they recognize that the dilemmas they face (such as those outlined in chapter 1) have no easy resolutions.

Leaders navigating AI deployment must acknowledge trade-offs openly, engage diverse voices in decision-making and build governance structures that embed ethics from the start. The UK's ambition cannot rest on rhetoric, sector silos or sporadic peaks of innovation. Authentic leadership requires integrating lessons across boundaries and redefining 'success' as sustainable transformation, not first-mover advantage.

Systemic barriers: the recurring patterns

The pilot trap described in chapter 2 is not abstract. Across every sector examined above, the same pattern is visible: controlled experiments that succeed under favourable conditions, but then stall when confronting the institutional realities of scale. The risk is creating what might be called 'demonstration-ware'; impressive showcases that never achieve the unglamorous work of operating reliably under real-world constraints. What follows identifies the systemic barriers that produce this pattern.

The barriers identified here are not inevitable features of organizational life. They are the accumulated result of decades of institutional choices that can, with sufficient courage and clarity, be unmade and remade. The question is whether UK leaders are prepared to acknowledge how deep the required changes must go.

Governance fragmentation

The governance fragmentation and procurement barriers diagnosed in chapter 2 manifest across every sector examined above. What the sectoral evidence adds is specificity: it reveals exactly where fragmentation creates the most acute bottlenecks, and where the greatest leverage for reform exists.

Policy without coordinated enforcement

A pattern emerges across the case studies: policies are created, but implementation enforcement varies dramatically. This gap becomes acute in AI governance, where regulatory divergence between the UK, EU and US creates operational challenges for organizations working across jurisdictions.

The UK passed the Data (Use and Access) Act 2025 to protect data while reducing reporting burdens.[7] Yet the Law Society noted that, while the act supports innovation, 'there must be safeguards and protections for using personal data and publicly available content'.[8] Simultaneously, the UK renamed its AI Safety Institute to the AI Security Institute in February 2025, signalling a shift in focus from bias and discrimination toward security.[9] These signals highlight changing priorities but create ambiguity: which concerns are regulators prioritizing?

This gap between policy creation and implementation clarity undermines legitimacy and effectiveness. When policies vary dramatically in how they are interpreted, resourced and enforced across sectors and regions, neither innovators nor citizens can trust the system. The UK risks getting the worst of both worlds: the innovation-dampening perception of heavy regulation without the citizen-protecting reality of effective enforcement.

Chapter 4 proposes a specific institutional response: a multi-stakeholder governance forum with mandated participation and a statutory AI Coordination Authority with powers modelled on the Office for Budget Responsibility.

Reality check: coordination means giving up autonomy

Every review of UK digital fragmentation reaches the same conclusion: we need better coordination. We need cross-departmental alignment; sectoral regulatory coherence;

shared standards and infrastructure; central–local cooperation. The diagnosis is correct and repeated endlessly. What is rarely acknowledged is what coordination actually requires: organizations with current autonomy must surrender it.

The NHS trust that has developed its own digital systems must adopt national standards that constrain local choice. The financial regulator that has established its own AI governance approach must align with principles it did not design. The local authority that has built relationships with preferred vendors must participate in national procurement frameworks. The government department that has created its own data architecture must migrate to shared platforms. Each organization faces the same calculation: coordination offers collective benefits but demands individual sacrifice.

This is why coordination initiatives consistently fail. Organizations publicly support coordination while privately protecting their autonomy. They attend coordination meetings, sign collaborative agreements and endorse shared principles. Then they continue operating as before, citing unique circumstances that require local flexibility. The rationale is always reasonable: 'Our context is different. Our users have specific needs. Our regulatory environment has particular requirements. We support coordination in principle but this specific standard doesn't work for us.'

The result is coordination as theatre. Working groups that produce documents no one implements. Shared platforms that remain optional. Standards that every organization 'substantially complies with' through their own unique interpretation. The appearance of coordination without the reality of constraint.

The uncomfortable choice for UK leaders: create coordination mechanisms with real enforcement power, accepting the political cost of overriding organizational autonomy, or continue producing coordination strategies that organizations politely ignore. The current approach of encouraging voluntary alignment through persuasion and incentives has not worked and shows no signs of working. The question is whether leaders are willing to exercise the authority that coordination requires or whether fragmentation is simply the price the UK pays for preserving organizational independence.

Incentives that punish adaptation

The UK's institutional incentive structures systematically discourage the behaviours transformation requires. Risk aversion is rewarded; experimentation is punished. Short-term metrics dominate; long-term capability-building is deprioritized. Individual accountability trumps collective responsibility; collaboration is nice-to-have rather than structurally embedded.

Consider the incentives facing a senior civil servant contemplating a bold AI pilot. If the pilot fails publicly, their career suffers; if it succeeds quietly, credit flows elsewhere. Funding is annual and competitive, making multiyear investments nearly impossible. Procurement frameworks favour established vendors and proven technologies, not experimental partnerships. Success is measured by on-time, on-budget delivery of specified outputs, not by learning, adaptation or long-term outcomes.

The rational response is caution, with a focus on small, safe projects that meet formal requirements without challenging structural constraints. Innovation becomes confined to protected spaces in labs, sandboxes and pilot programmes, insulated from the broader system and therefore unable to transform it.

Consequently, incentive redesign is central to institutional adaptation. This means rewarding learning through performance frameworks that value lesson-capture and knowledge-sharing, not just successful outcomes. It means derisking experimentation through 'safe-to-fail' spaces where teams can test ideas without career jeopardy. It means aligning time horizons through multiyear budgets and evaluation cycles that match transformation timescales. And it means embedding collaboration through funding mechanisms that require cross-organizational partnerships and reward collective outcomes.

Inclusion as episodic performance

The UK's commitment to inclusion is real in principle but variable in practice. Consultations occur at the start of major initiatives, stakeholder workshops accompany strategy launches and diversity statistics appear in annual reports. Yet meaningful participation in which affected communities shape decisions, not just react to them, remains rare.

The result is that digital transformation repeatedly amplifies existing inequalities. AI systems trained on biased data perpetuate discrimination. Digital services designed for urban professionals exclude rural communities. Automation strategies developed without worker input trigger defensive resistance.

True inclusion requires structural change: co-design from the start, with affected communities involved in problem definition and solution design; sustained engagement through long-term relationships extending beyond project timelines; resource redistribution providing funding and capacity-building support for grassroots organizations; and decision-making power through mechanisms that give communities real influence over choices that affect them.

Chapter 4 translates these requirements into Principle 3 (Authentic Inclusion), delivered through a Community-Embedded Innovation Lab model that roots innovation in specific places rather than imposing it from above.

Ethics as retrofitted afterthought

Ethical considerations in UK AI deployment are typically addressed late, reactive and peripheral. Ethics reviews occur after technical designs are finalized. Bias audits happen after systems are deployed. Fairness concerns emerge after public backlash forces renegotiation.

This retrofitted approach is structurally embedded. Technical teams operate under pressure to deliver quickly, with ethics seen as potential slowdown. Commercial vendors prioritize competitive advantages, treating transparency and accountability as regulatory compliance costs. Policymakers focus on economic competitiveness, framing ethical concerns as obstacles to overcome rather than design principles to embed.

Embedding ethics requires fundamental shifts by treating fairness, transparency and accountability as design principles integrated from the first stages of system design; building diverse design teams that include ethicists, social scientists and affected community representatives alongside engineers; conducting proactive bias testing that stress-tests for fairness across demographic groups before deployment; and ensuring transparent decision-making through public documentation of trade-offs, limitations and ethical choices.

The response of building real trust through transparency in design, accountability mechanisms and responsive governance is developed as chapter 4's second design principle and operationalized in the 'Ethical by Default' reforms it defines.

Reality check: the risk of digital veneer

There is a significant risk that AI adoption in the UK, particularly in the public sector, follows the same pattern as website adoption before it: a new technology layer placed on top of unreformed processes, creating the appearance of modernization without its substance.

The pattern is familiar. In the 2010s, government departments moved services online. Forms that had previously been completed on paper were made available as web forms.

Information that had been available in leaflets was published on web pages. The interface changed; the underlying processes, data architecture and policy logic frequently did not. GOV.UK now hosts thousands of forms. This is an achievement in digitization, but not necessarily in transformation. The policy processes behind those forms, the legislative logic they implement and the data systems they draw on remain in many cases unreformed.

The AI equivalent is already emerging. Organizations are deploying chatbots on top of existing websites, summarization tools on top of existing document stores and assistants on top of existing case management systems. In each case, the AI layer makes the existing system more accessible, but it does not make the existing system better. An LLM answering citizens' questions about a policy that is poorly designed does not improve the policy. A summarization tool compressing documents that contain contradictory guidance does not resolve the contradictions. A chatbot navigating a process that is unnecessarily complex does not simplify the process.

Worse, the AI layer can actually actively impede real reform. Once an organization has invested in an AI tool that makes a broken process tolerable, the case for fixing the underlying process weakens. The symptom has been treated; the cause persists. The veneer becomes permanent precisely because it is effective enough to reduce the pressure for structural change.

The alternative is to use AI first as an analytical tool to identify where duplication exists across legal frameworks, where data is fragmented across incompatible systems and where processes have accumulated unnecessary complexity. These insights can be used to rationalize and simplify before deploying AI as a citizen-facing interface. This sequencing requires institutional discipline. It is less visible, less politically attractive and slower to produce results than deploying a chatbot. But it is the difference between transformation and veneer.

Absence of learning systems

Perhaps the most fundamental barrier is the UK's institutional inability to learn systematically from experience. Lessons from past failures are documented but not institutionalized. Insights from successful pilots remain siloed rather than shared. Knowledge accumulated by front line teams evaporates when projects end or staff leave.

The result is repeated cycles of failure. The same mistakes are repeated across sectors and decades with over-centralization, under-consultation, inadequate user research, premature scaling and insufficient testing. Each time, the diagnosis is familiar, yet structural change remains elusive.

Learning systems require more than good intentions. They need institutional memory through knowledge management systems that capture and curate lessons across projects and time. They need feedback loops connecting policy design to operational experience, ensuring that strategies adapt to reality. They need psychological safety through cultures where admitting failure, raising concerns and challenging orthodoxy are valued, not punished. And they need communities of practice consisting of networks that enable practitioners to share insights and collectively build capability.

The UK's transformation challenge is not primarily technical or financial. It is cultural and institutional, requiring the building of organizations capable of continuous adaptation in a rapidly changing environment. Chapter 4's first design principle of adaptive capacity and the Adaptive Learning Institution model it proposes define the specific institutional mechanisms these requirements demand.

Conclusions: the implementation imperative

This chapter traced a sobering path from aspiration to reality. The UK possesses several strengths: world-class research institutions, innovative companies, deep expertise across critical sectors and leaders capable of bold vision. Multibillion pound infrastructure investments demonstrate international confidence in the UK's potential.

Yet at every turn, ambition encounters institutional barriers that prevent transformation from taking root. The pattern is consistent across sectors and decades. While the UK excels at diagnosing what needs to change, developing sophisticated strategies for change and launching initiatives to drive change, it repeatedly fails at the sustained institutional adaptation required to make change durable.

This is not primarily a technical problem or a resource constraint. It is fundamentally about institutional capacity and whether organizations can develop the governance structures, incentive systems, cultural practices and learning mechanisms that transformation demands.

Leverage points for change

The systemic barriers identified in this chapter are not uniformly distributed. Different sectors face different constraints; different interventions create different leverage. Several high-leverage areas could reshape outcomes across the digital economy.

- *Government procurement and standards-setting,* which ripple through every sector.

- *NHS data governance and clinical engagement,* which could establish templates for responsible AI.

- *Education and skills infrastructure,* which determines future capacity.

- *Regional innovation ecosystems,* which could distribute capability beyond the 'golden triangle' of London, Cambridge and Oxford.

Yet the deeper question is not where to intervene but whether UK institutions can develop the adaptive capacity that sustained transformation requires.

Can UK institutions become adaptive?

The evidence from this chapter suggests that adaptive institutions share several characteristics. They need structural features: modular design that enables experimentation without destabilizing core operations; permeable boundaries that allow knowledge and resources to flow across organizational divides; and redundancy that provides a buffer for innovation and recovery from failure.

They need cultural attributes: psychological safety where raising concerns and challenging orthodoxy is valued; learning orientation where capturing and sharing lessons is rewarded; and a collaborative ethos where collective success matters more than individual credit.

They need governance mechanisms: distributed authority with clear accountability; transparent decision-making with documented trade-offs; and participatory processes that give affected communities real influence.

And they need resource strategies: multiyear funding that matches transformation timescales; flexible budgets that enable adaptation as understanding evolves; and investment in capability, not just delivery.

Few UK institutions currently exhibit these characteristics. Yet examples exist. GDS at its peak proved that small, empowered teams with protected mandates can drive true innovation. Open Banking showed how regulatory courage and multistakeholder collaboration could reshape an entire sector. Regional Covid-19 responses revealed how local leaders, given autonomy and resources, could adapt faster than centralized bureaucracies. These examples prove adaptation is possible. The question is whether such successes can become the norm rather than exceptional.

It is reasonable to ask whether the core problem is that AI implementation teams staffed by junior analysts on temporary contracts is a barrier to long-term success. However, the staffing problem is more likely a symptom, not a cause. Junior staffing reflects a governance structure that treats AI as a technology project rather than an institutional transformation. Temporary contracts reflect a procurement system that outsources capability rather than building it. The absence of senior technical leadership reflects a skills pipeline that has never produced enough people with both technical depth and institutional authority.

The barriers diagnosed above require institutional remedies of corresponding focus and detail. Each barrier maps to a concrete design response proposed in chapter 4: governance fragmentation demands a multistakeholder governance forum with enforcement powers and a statutory coordination authority; perverse incentives require adaptive learning institutions with cross-functional teams, failure documentation and multi-year budgets; episodic inclusion must be replaced by authentic participation, resourced from the start through community-embedded innovation labs; retrofitted ethics gives way to deep trust built through transparency in design, accountability mechanisms and managed transitions; and the absence of learning systems calls for adaptive capacity via distributed decision-making, embedded feedback loops and tolerance for failure as a condition of progress. These are not abstract aspirations, but they require specific principles, governance models and actionable reforms.

CHAPTER 4

Adapting the UK's institutions

The preceding chapters established that the UK's transformation challenges are institutional, not technological. This chapter turns from diagnosis to design and asks the following question: how must governance, incentives and organizational practice change to enable the adaptive capacity that AI deployment demands? It concludes that the UK's AI strategy depends on fundamental redesign of its governance, incentive structures and organizational practices.

This chapter offers that codification across four levels. First, three guiding principles – adaptive capacity, deep trust and authentic inclusion – that should underpin all institutional reform. Second, infrastructure design requirements and sovereign compute strategy that translate principles into technical architecture. Third, institutional structures – three governance models – and blueprints for reform across government, business and civil society. Finally, a sequencing framework for implementing these reforms is defined, and elaborated in detail in chapter 8.

Introduction: from barriers to blueprints

Delivering on the UK's AI ambitions will require a bold approach. System redesign is not incremental improvement. It is not adding new initiatives, new committees or new funding streams to the existing architecture. Redesign requires rethinking foundational elements: how do institutions make decisions? Who has a voice? What do we measure and reward? How do we learn from failure? How do we embed inclusion from the start?

The good news is that the blueprints exist. Across the UK and internationally, innovative organizations have made significant progress in adaptive governance, inclusion and embedded learning. The work ahead is not to invent new models from scratch but to extract what works from these examples, codify the principles and make them systemic.

This chapter offers that codification. It outlines the following:

- design principles that should underpin UK digital governance (adaptive capacity, real trust and authentic inclusion);
- governance models providing institutional structures and decision-making processes that embody these principles;
- practical blueprints for implementation, including specific reforms to regulation, incentive structures and organizational practice; and
- transition pathways: how to move from current fragmented practice to the integrated, adaptive system the UK needs.

Three guiding principles: adaptive capacity, deep trust and authentic inclusion

The UK's prescribed approach to AI governance represents a distinctive principles-based regulatory strategy that differs from both US (deregulatory) and EU (comprehensive legislative) models.[1] Rather than creating new AI-specific legislation or regulatory bodies, the UK framework emphasizes five high-level principles that existing sectoral regulators are expected to implement.

1. *Safety, security and robustness.* Systems must be demonstrably safe and resilient.

2. *Appropriate transparency and explainability.* Decision-making must be explainable to affected parties.

3. *Fairness.* Systems must avoid discrimination and ensure equitable treatment.

4. *Accountability and governance.* There must be clear lines of responsibility for system outcomes.

5. *Contestability and redress.* There must be meaningful mechanisms for affected individuals to challenge decisions.

The UK's principles-based regulatory approach – organized around safety, transparency, fairness, accountability and contestability – provides a foundation. But regulatory principles alone do not redesign institutions. Three deeper design principles must guide reform and shape the redesign of UK institutions.

Principle 1: adaptive capacity

The absence of learning systems diagnosed in chapter 3, where lessons from failure evaporate, knowledge remains siloed and repeated cycles of the same mistakes persist across decades, calls for a fundamentally different institutional capability. Adaptive capacity is the organizational ability to sense change in the environment, interpret what it means, and adjust strategy and practice in response.

1. Adaptive capacity

The ability to sense change and adjust strategy in response. Requires distributed decision making, feedback loops and tolerance for failure.

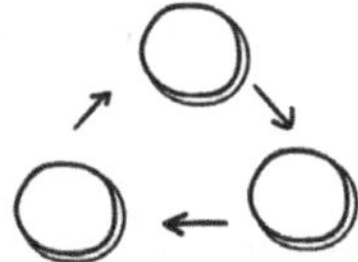

2. Deep trust

Rebuilt through transparency in design, clear accountability for harms and inclusive deliberation with affected communities.

3. Authentic inclusion

Integrating diverse perspectives and decision making power from the start, ensuring benefits are distributed across all regions and communities.

Figure 3. Redesigning UK institutions for the AI era: principles, structures and reforms.

Adaptive capacity requires the following.

- *Distributed decision-making.* Not all authority concentrated at the centre, but decisions made as close as possible to where change is happening and where consequences are felt.
- *Feedback loops.* Regular, honest conversations with users, affected communities and front line staff. Not surveys or focus groups conducted annually, but embedded, continuous feedback.
- *Iterative learning.* The assumption that initial strategies will be incomplete or wrong. Building in regular review points, learning from experience, course correction without shame or blame.

- *Tolerance for failure.* The recognition that some experiments will fail. The goal is not to avoid failure but to fail fast, learn quickly and apply those lessons at scale.

- *Investment in capability.* Not just in technology or short-term projects, but in building durable human capability (talent, expertise and networks) that enables sustained adaptation.

Principle 2: deep trust

When ethics is treated as a retrofitted afterthought and is addressed late, reactive and peripheral, as chapter 3's analysis documented, then the result is a predictable erosion of public confidence. Trust in digital institutions has eroded. Citizens worry about data misuse, algorithmic bias and the concentration of power. Trust can only be rebuilt if digital governance practices become transparent, accountable and genuinely responsive to public concerns.

Deep trust requires the following.

- *Transparency in design.* Opening the process of designing digital systems to scrutiny. Not hiding how algorithms are built, how decisions are made or how data is used. Publishing the code, the training data and the performance metrics.

- *Accountability.* Creating clear mechanisms for redress when things go wrong. If a person is harmed by an algorithmic decision, they should be able to challenge it, understand why it was made and get a correction. This is not just a technical fix but a governance transformation.

- *Responsive to evidence.* Building institutions that listen to research about AI harms, that change practice in response to evidence of bias or injustice and that do not wait for failure to act.

- *Inclusive deliberation.* Involving the affected communities in the conversation about digital governance. Not asking them to ratify decisions made elsewhere but appropriately incorporating their knowledge and values into how systems are designed, deployed and evaluated.

- *Managed transitions.* When technologies have negative consequences, creating structures to support affected people through transition. If automation displaces workers, are they supported in reskilling? If algorithmic systems are biased, how are harms remedied?

Principle 3: authentic inclusion

Chapter 3 identified a recurring pattern: inclusion as episodic performance, where consultations occur at the start of initiatives but affected communities have no sustained influence over design or governance. The remedy must go beyond better consultation. Inclusion is often treated as a box to check. Authentic inclusion means something deeper: the true integration of diverse perspectives, experiences and decision-making power into how digital institutions operate.

Authentic inclusion requires the following.

- *From the start, not as retrofit.* Including diverse voices and perspectives in design, not bolting on consultation after decisions are made.

- *Power, not just voice.* Ensuring that the people most affected by digital systems, not just technology experts or policymakers, have real influence over how those systems are designed and governed.

- *Distributed across scales.* Inclusion at the individual level (via co-design with users), organizational level (through diverse teams), system level (with representation from different communities in governance bodies) and societal level (by ensuring that transformation serves all regions and communities).

- *Resourced adequately.* Authentic inclusion is not free. It takes time, expertise and facilitation. Institutions that commit to it must resource it properly, not as an afterthought budget item.
- *Measured and course-corrected.* Building in regular assessments: are the people included being heard? Are their recommendations being adopted? If not, why not? What needs to change?

Infrastructure: from design requirements to sovereign compute

Drawing on international evidence from established digital leaders such as Estonia and India, four critical design requirements emerge for building digital infrastructure capable of supporting AI deployment at scale.

Mandate interoperability and ecosystem design

Drawing on experiences in other nations, the UK must prioritize interoperability and coordination of its AI systems. For example, the utility of India's digital technology stack is not a single application, but its seamless integration across identity, payments and data layers. Similarly, the power of Estonia's X-Road digital platform is not the underlying technology, but the fact that all government systems are mandatorily interoperable. For the UK, this means ensuring deep integration not only across government departments but also with the private sector.

The design must mandate that all systems can exchange verified data, that citizens' information flows seamlessly across public and private services and that no critical information lives in isolated silos. This is the opposite of the fragmented approach that has characterized much UK government IT spending in the past.

Embed trust and privacy by design

Privacy and security must be fundamental design requirements, not afterthoughts or compliance burdens. In digitally mature nations such as Estonia, public trust is built through radical transparency that allows citizens to track exactly which officials and systems access their data, as well as when and why. This creates accountability, which in turn inspires confidence.

Critically, transparency about data access is not a privacy violation. Rather, it is the mechanism for ensuring privacy is respected. Citizens who can see exactly what happens to their data are more likely to trust the system and provide the information it needs to work effectively.

Deliver tangible public value from day one

Digital transformation is accelerated when delivering immediate, visible efficiency gains. UK initiatives that struggled often imposed burdens before delivering benefits. This requirement encourages starting small by demonstrating value with clear benefits to drive adoption before scaling.

For example, the now-decommissioned GOV.UK Verify struggled because it required citizens to undergo a rigorous, often failure-prone identity check before they could access any service, creating a 'friction-heavy' entry point with no immediate reward.[2] In contrast, the NHS App succeeded by leading with a high-value, low-friction feature: repeat prescriptions.[3] In solving a tangible 'pain point' by eliminating the need to call a GP surgery or visit in person, the government earned the 'permission' from the public to introduce more complex features such as medical record access and organ donation registration.

Design for digital Inclusion, not digital exclusion

This is perhaps the most critical requirement for the UK context. Universal Credit's 'digital by default' design, analysed in chapter 2, demonstrated that excluding vulnerable populations from digital services is not a minor implementation failure but a breach of fundamental governance principles. Any new digital system must therefore include

- robust offline alternatives for those without digital access,
- human support for those unable to navigate digital interfaces,
- comprehensive testing against edge cases and vulnerable populations,
- clear audit trails and appeals processes for automated decisions, and
- explicit design to avoid recreating or amplifying historical biases in data.

When technology fails or access is limited, vulnerable populations suffer profound hardship. This risk of exclusion is the critical failure point that the UK's own history (specifically the Universal Credit rollout) underscores.

Reality check: agile governance requires political courage

Adaptive, experimental governance sounds appealing in principle. In practice, it requires political leaders accepting something democratic systems typically punish: visible failure. Pilots will reveal misunderstandings and errors. Experiments will produce results that contradict prior commitments. In such cases, learning requires acknowledging when initial assumptions were wrong.

Yet political incentives reward certainty, consistency and the appearance of control. Ministers who admit that a policy experiment failed face accusations of incompetence. Civil servants who change course based on evidence get criticized for U-turns. Opposition parties weaponize adaptation as proof of chaos. Until these political dynamics change, 'agile governance' will remain largely aspirational and permitted in small, low-visibility contexts but abandoned when stakes rise or media attention intensifies. The UK's ability to govern using AI adaptively depends less on adopting new frameworks than on creating political space for honest experimentation, including accepting failure as a key part of the learning process. Without this cultural shift, governance will remain rigid regardless of what policy documents promise.

Sovereign compute and resilient infrastructure

A fair challenge to this book's emphasis on regional AI infrastructure is that geography should be irrelevant to computing. A neural network runs the same mathematics whether the server sits in Sunderland or San Jose. The mathematical logic behind AI models is independent of the physical servers used to run them. If 'computing as utility' was the insight that made AI economically viable by offering processing power available anywhere, anytime, at declining marginal cost, then regionalism appears to swim against the technological current.

This challenge is technically correct but strategically incomplete. What geography determines is not how AI processes, but who governs the processing, under what law, with what recourse and subject to whose oversight. When a UK citizen's NHS data is processed by an algorithm running on infrastructure owned by a US hyperscaler, the mathematics are identical regardless of location. But the enforcement power, legal jurisdiction, audit rights and practical ability to halt a malfunctioning system are entirely dependent on where that infrastructure sits, who owns it, and what contractual and regulatory levers UK institutions retain.[4]

'Regional AI' in this book therefore means three specific things.

1. *Data residency.* Ensuring that sensitive public-sector data in health, justice, welfare and national security is stored and processed within jurisdictions where UK law applies and UK regulators can intervene without requiring foreign consent.

2. *Infrastructure as an accountability lever.* Building and maintaining domestic compute capacity so that the UK retains a credible alternative if foreign-owned platforms change their terms, are subject to conflicting legal demands or fail.

3. *Skills ecosystems rooted in place.* Using AI Growth Zones not merely as data centre real estate but as focal points where universities, public agencies and local businesses develop shared capability, thus ensuring that AI's economic benefits reach Manchester, Edinburgh and the North East, not just the 'golden triangle'.

In practice, digital sovereignty becomes tangible when leaders make decisions about infrastructure. Choices about where data is stored, how AI workloads are run and who controls critical systems will shape the UK's room for manoeuvre in the AI era for a decade or more. For UK institutions, sovereignty is not an abstract ideal; it is encoded in architecture diagrams, procurement contracts, and the governance of data centres and supercomputers.

The UK's emerging strategy recognizes this. The AI Opportunities Action Plan[5] and the UK Compute Roadmap[6] both highlight the need for 'sovereign, secure and sustainable' AI compute as a foundation for growth and resilience. Sovereign compute, in this context, means capacity that is either owned by the public sector or contractually controlled so it can be allocated quickly and independently to national priorities. Alongside this, a broader portfolio of domestic and international compute capability (including commercial cloud and international partnerships) will continue to play a role but cannot substitute for a core infrastructure that UK institutions can direct on their own terms.

The scale of these commitments deserves scrutiny. The 2025 Spending Review allocated £2 billion to AI infrastructure over four years, including approximately £1 billion for the AI Research Resource (AIRR), £500 million for a new Sovereign AI Unit and £750 million for a national supercomputer at the University of Edinburgh. The Compute Roadmap targets a twenty-fold expansion of publicly accessible AI compute by 2030 and envisions 6 GW of AI-capable data centre capacity. These are significant commitments by UK standards. Placed in the global context, however, the UK currently holds approximately 1.3% of the world's compute capacity. Hyperscale companies committed more than $300 billion globally to AI infrastructure in 2025 alone. The US Stargate programme, a single public–private venture, represents $100 billion. The question is not whether the UK's investment is welcome (it is), but whether it is sufficient to deliver the sovereign capability the strategy describes, or whether it represents the minimum viable foundation that must be supplemented by sustained annual commitment across multiple spending review cycles.

The sovereignty provisions proposed in this book (data residency requirements, exit pathways, audit access and jurisdiction clauses) must also reckon with the reality of the UK's negotiating position. The £250 billion in cross-Atlantic investment is based on terms shaped primarily by the investing companies, not by the UK government. Imposing sovereignty conditions that materially increase costs or slow deployment risks redirecting investment to competing jurisdictions. The practical approach is therefore not to demand sovereignty as a blanket precondition but to negotiate it contract by contract, prioritizing the most sensitive functions (such as health data, justice, welfare and national security) and accepting lighter-touch provisions elsewhere. Sovereignty by default is the direction of travel; sovereignty in every contract from day one is not achievable. What matters is that every major AI infrastructure agreement includes at minimum: a data residency clause for specified categories of sensitive data, a documented exit pathway with defined migration timescales and costs, and audit access provisions that give UK regulators meaningful visibility into how systems operate. These are commercially standard provisions in other regulated sectors. The challenge is not legal novelty but institutional willingness to insist on them when large investment figures create pressure to sign quickly.

The sovereign compute argument must also reckon with the 'DeepSeek moment'. In January 2025, China's DeepSeek demonstrated that a reasoning model trained for less than $6 million could match systems costing orders of magnitude more, by prioritizing compute efficiency over compute scale.[7] If this trajectory continues (and the subsequent proliferation of efficient 'distilled' models suggests it will), then the UK's relatively modest compute investment could prove more strategically viable than raw numbers suggest, provided the emphasis is placed on how this capability is used responsibly and effectively. This means investing as heavily in AI research talent who can innovate on efficiency as in the hardware itself. Sovereign compute remains essential for data residency, audit capability and crisis resilience. But the efficiency revolution means that 'sovereign' need not mean 'matching hyperscale'.

AI Growth Zones, national supercomputing centres and specialized AI research facilities are the institutional vehicles for realizing this vision. They are intended to anchor large-scale AI infrastructure in specific regions, unlock investment in data centres and provide test beds where new chips and architectures can be trialled under UK regulatory oversight. When designed well, they do more than host hardware. They become focal points for skills, standards and shared services. Essentially, they become places where universities, start-ups, public agencies and regulators learn together how to deploy powerful compute safely, efficiently and inclusively.

Delivering this kind of infrastructure at scale demands a shift in design principles. First, UK institutions must prioritize infrastructure control before AI system control. If governments and regulators do not have credible access to the data and infrastructure layers, they will struggle to enforce transparency, audit obligations or safety constraints on any AI system running above them.

Second, systems should be built around multivendor, exit-friendly architectures. That means avoiding single-provider lock-in, using open standards, and designing workloads so they can be moved between on-premises, sovereign and commercial environments without prohibitive cost or disruption.

Third, leaders must be explicit about data localization for sensitive functions. For sectors such as health, justice, welfare and critical infrastructure, the ability to insist that data is stored and processed within UK or devolved jurisdictions is not just symbolic; it directly shapes enforcement power, redress and public trust.

Fourth, infrastructure planning must treat resilience and crisis response as first-order requirements. This involves asking what happens if foreign cloud services are disrupted, sanctioned or made subject to conflicting legal demands, then, based on the answers, building contingency options so critical AI systems can continue operating effectively via reconfigurable platforms.

For central government, these principles imply that procurement, industrial strategy and the AI Opportunities Action Plan need to be aligned so that a growing share of public AI workloads can, where necessary, run on sovereign or audit-capable infrastructure. Business cases for major programmes should require teams to justify not only functionality and cost, but also where data will live, how easily workloads can be moved, and what rights the UK has to inspect and intervene in the underlying systems. For organizations such as NHS trusts, local authorities, regulators and arms-length bodies, infrastructure sovereignty should become part of everyday due diligence: which jurisdiction applies if something goes wrong? Who can access logs and models? How quickly can we migrate if trust is lost?

For regional leaders, AI Growth Zones and related investments are an opportunity to build lasting local capability, not merely to host foreign facilities. This means tying infrastructure to skills pipelines, local innovation ecosystems and shared public-sector platforms, rather than treating it as a stand-alone property development. If the UK succeeds, sovereign compute and resilient infrastructure will not be a defensive posture, but a source of advantage: enabling faster, safer and more inclusive deployment of AI at scale, with the confidence that the systems shaping national life remain, ultimately, under UK control.

What sovereign compute success looks like by 2030

Measurable sovereign compute capability would include all sensitive public-sector AI workloads in health, justice, welfare and national security running on infrastructure where UK law applies and UK regulators can intervene without foreign consent; a credible domestic alternative (not necessarily equivalent in scale, but functionally sufficient) to at least one hyperscale provider for critical public services; contractual exit provisions in all major cloud procurement that allow workload migration within twelve months; and a public reporting mechanism that tracks, annually, what percentage of government AI workloads run on sovereign, audit-capable infrastructure versus foreign-controlled platforms. Without such metrics, 'sovereignty' remains an aspiration rather than an accountable commitment.

Institutional structures: three governance models

The previous sections established what adaptive institutions must achieve: meaningful inclusion, embedded ethics, continuous learning and coordinated action across boundaries. But principles alone do not create change. They must be embodied in concrete institutional structures that make new behaviours the default rather than the exception.

To achieve this requires that design principles drive concrete institutional changes. Three governance models can guide such reform.

Model 1: the adaptive learning institution

Two of the barriers diagnosed in chapter 3 (incentive structures that punish adaptation and the absence of learning systems) converge on a single institutional requirement: organizations must be redesigned around learning rather than compliance. The adaptive learning institution organizes itself around continuous learning and improvement. The key features are as follows.

- *Cross-functional teams* rather than siloed departments (with IT separate from policy, and policy separate from operations), which bring together technologists, policymakers, front line staff, affected communities and ethicists.

- *Regular review cycles* of what is working, what is not and what needs to change. These are not just management meetings but spaces where diverse perspectives are appropriately considered.

- *Failure documentation and learning* for projects that falter or systems that cause harm to extract and codify lessons, not to hide failure. These lessons are actively shared across the organization and beyond.

- *Investment in the capability* to fund not just projects but people. This includes funding for training, for sabbaticals, for time to experiment and for cross-organizational learning networks.

- *External accountability* via regular public reporting on what the institution learned, how it changed practice and what results emerged.

The NHS Digital Academy provides a working example. By focusing clinical and technical leaders to work jointly on current transformation challenges, rather than teaching abstract principles, it builds capability grounded in specific institutional contexts. Participants do not learn about digital transformation; they transform their own organizations with expert support. The model works because learning is embedded in delivery, not separated from it. An AI equivalent might embed cross-disciplinary teams (data scientists, policy professionals, front line staff, ethicists) within departments working on live AI deployments, with a mandate to publish lessons (including failures) quarterly.

Many of these initiatives are already in place to varying degrees across government agencies and other organizations. The task is to make their adoption systemic.

Model 2: the multistakeholder governance forum

The governance fragmentation diagnosed in chapter 3, where policy is created but enforcement varies dramatically, and coordination becomes theatre rather than constraint, requires an institutional structure that makes coordination binding rather than voluntary. Many of the UK's digital challenges cannot be solved by single institutions but instead require coordination across government, business, civil society, academia and affected communities. Initiatives such as Multi-Stakeholder

Governance Forums (as used in the Open Banking initiative[8]) are examples of ways to manage such coordination. Their key features include the following.

- *Represented participation.* Government, business, civil society, academia and affected communities each have a voice in governing digital strategy and practice.
- *Shared agenda-setting.* Priorities are not set by government and handed down but developed through deliberation among stakeholders.
- *Resource pooling.* Different stakeholders contribute resources (e.g. funding, expertise, convening power) toward shared goals.
- *Regular accountability.* Participants are accountable to each other and to the public for progress.
- *Distributed action.* Rather than centralizing all implementation, stakeholders commit to action within their spheres. For example, government reforms its procurement, business commits to ethical AI practices and civil society ensures that marginalized communities' voices are heard.

Open Banking's implementation entity provides the clearest UK precedent. It succeeded because participation was not voluntary but mandated by the Competition and Markets Authority, stakeholders had defined roles with accountability for delivery (not merely attendance) and progress was measured against published milestones with consequences for nondelivery. An AI governance forum designed on the same principles of mandated participation, published milestones and consequences for nondelivery would differ fundamentally from the consultative bodies the UK typically establishes.

The UK's Smart Data programme, coordinated through the Smart Data Council within the Department for Science, Innovation and Technology, offers a live demonstration of this approach. It is arguably the most sophisticated experiment in governed data-sharing currently operating in the UK, bringing together regulators, industry, consumer representatives and government in a structured framework that enables data portability and interoperability while maintaining appropriate protections. The programme provides practical evidence that the multistakeholder governance model advocated here is not theoretical; it is operational, imperfect and evolving in real time. Its experience offers valuable lessons for any AI governance framework that requires data to flow across institutional boundaries.

A variety of independent organizations have already taken steps to set up spaces for multistakeholder dialogue on AI governance. The task is to institutionalize these spaces and give them real decision-making power.

Model 3: the community-embedded innovation lab

Many promising digital innovations emerge at the local level in specific communities, organizations or neighbourhoods. Yet they struggle to scale because they lack connection to resources, policy support or broader learning networks. Efforts to establish community-embedded innovation centres can be useful for supporting and scaling local activities that would otherwise fail to be recognized. Their essential features include the following.

- *Rooted in communities.* Rather than top-down innovation centres, labs that are embedded in specific places, working on challenges identified by those communities.

- *Resources and support.* Providing funding, expertise and policy support to local innovators without imposing directives from above.

- *Connection to a broader network.* Linking local innovators to each other, to research and to policy, so that learning can flow in both directions (from local practice to policy and from policy/research back to local practice).

- *Measurement of real impact.* Assessing not just whether projects were implemented but whether they improved outcomes for the communities they serve.

- *Scaling pathways.* Clear mechanisms for scaling innovations that work beyond the original community.

The Connected Places Catapult's work with local authorities on transport data, and Nesta's partnership with councils on predictive analytics for children's services, offer partial precedents. Both demonstrate that innovation embedded in specific places and problems produces more transferable learning than top-down demonstration projects. The critical gap in both cases was a systematic mechanism for scaling what worked to other localities. A national network of AI Innovation Labs, perhaps five to ten, aligned with the AI Growth Zones with a shared learning platform and dedicated scaling support would address this gap.

These and several further examples offer a path forwards. These include local government digital pioneers, community organizations experimenting with social technology and civil society groups using data for social good. The task is to resource these institutions and connect them into a coherent system.

Blueprints for reform: government, business and civil society

The governance models described above (adaptive learning institutions, multistakeholder forums and community-centred design) offer frameworks for how UK institutions could operate differently. But models remain theoretical until they are embedded in the specific rules, structures and practices that shape daily decisions.

Hence, it is essential to acknowledge that the gap between aspiration and implementation diagnosed in chapter 3 applies equally to institutional reform itself. Without concrete operational changes, even the best governance frameworks become yet another set of principles that organizations endorse in theory while continuing business as usual in practice. Progress demands that governance models are embedded into specific, actionable reforms across government, business, civil society and the mechanisms that connect them.

Government reform

Government processes and structures are often the bottleneck in UK digital transformation. Specific reforms to be considered include the following.

Agile procurement

The Procurement Act 2023 (effective from February 2025) introduces new competitive flexible procedures and permits innovation partnerships.[9] These are both mechanisms that enable the iterative approach this book advocates. The challenge is not legislative authority but institutional practice: contracting officers trained in the old framework, audit bodies expecting detailed upfront specifications and established contractors whose business models depend on large fixed-price deals.

Specific reforms could include

- mandating that all AI procurement above a threshold value (e.g. £500,000) uses a competitive flexible procedure with built-in review stages rather than traditional single-award contracts;

- requiring 'exit-by-design' provisions in all AI platform contracts, with maximum twelve-month migration pathways and escrowed source code or model weights for custom systems;

- establishing a cross-government AI Procurement Centre of Expertise (modelled on the Crown Commercial Service's existing category teams) with the authority to preapprove framework agreements for common AI use cases, reducing the procurement burden on individual departments; and

- piloting outcome-based contracts in two or three departments where payment is linked to measurable service improvement rather than delivery of specified outputs.

The UK Digital Marketplace (formerly G-Cloud) provides the infrastructure;[10] what is needed is the institutional permission to use it differently.

Cross-departmental governance

The UK currently has multiple bodies with partial AI remits, including the AI Safety Institute, the Sovereign AI Unit, the Department for Science, Innovation and Technology's digital directorate, the Central Digital and Data Office, sectoral regulators and the Geospatial Commission, among others. What is missing is a single body with authority to resolve conflicts between departments, enforce common standards and allocate shared resources.

The fragmentation extends to regulatory activity: the Competition and Markets Authority, the Financial Conduct Authority (FCA), the Information Commissioner's Office (ICO) and Ofcom (collectively the Digital Regulation Cooperation Forum) have each published AI-specific guidance, and in June 2025 the FCA and ICO announced a joint statutory code of practice for AI – the first move toward binding AI-specific rules within the UK's regulatory framework.[11] These are welcome initiatives, but they underscore the need for coordination: four regulators pursuing four approaches to the same technology, with a coordination forum that has no binding authority over its members.

One way to achieve this is via a statutory AI Coordination Authority. Not a new regulator, but a body with defined powers modelled on the precedent of the Office for Budget Responsibility: independent of departmental interests, with a statutory mandate and required to publish regular assessments of national AI readiness. Its minimum powers should include

- authority to mandate cross-departmental data-sharing agreements for AI applications affecting multiple departments;
- power to conduct and publish AI readiness assessments for all major government departments, with departments required to respond publicly;
- authority to set and enforce technical interoperability standards for government AI systems; and
- convening power to resolve disputes between sectoral regulators interpreting AI principles differently.

The critical design choice is between a body that coordinates (convenes, recommends, publishes) and one that directs (mandates, enforces, allocates). The UK's experience suggests that coordination without enforcement produces the 'strategies that organizations politely ignore' diagnosed in chapter 3. However, a body with directive power requires primary legislation and faces departmental resistance. The pragmatic path may be to establish such a body first under prerogative powers with coordination and transparency functions, then seek statutory authority once the body has demonstrated value – the trajectory GDS itself followed before its mandate was absorbed back into departmental structures.

Talent mobility
This entails creating mechanisms that enable talent to move between the government, the private sector, academia and civil society. Government should be able to recruit top talent from Silicon Valley or academia; people should be able to move between sectors without sacrificing their pension or seniority.

Learning investment
This includes a budget for government to invest in its own learning in areas such as training for civil servants in agile practice, data science and ethical AI; sabbaticals for deep learning; and time for communities of practice to meet and learn from each other.

Business and industry reform

Business also needs to shift. Specific reforms identified include the following.

- *Stakeholder governance.* Large technology companies and other digital leaders should establish governance structures that include worker representation, affected communities, civil society and ethics experts, not just shareholders.

- *Ethical by default.* Companies should commit to designing AI systems with ethical safeguards built in from the start, not retrofitted. This includes practices such as algorithmic impact assessment, bias testing and transparent documentation.

- *Skills and inclusion.* Companies should commit to using their scale and resources to build digital skills and opportunity across the UK, not just recruiting top talent. This could include apprenticeship programs, community training partnerships and commitment to hiring from underrepresented groups.

- *Transparency.* Companies should commit to transparency about how their systems work, what data they use and what harms have been identified. This includes publishing diversity data, algorithmic audits and evidence of bias.

Civil society and community reform

Civil society and communities have often been on the receiving end of digital transformation. Increasing their input and involvement requires specific reforms, including the following.

- *Community advisory councils.* Public agencies and digital platforms should establish community advisory councils that have a real voice in governance and resource decisions.

- *Data commons.* Communities should have access to data about their own regions on topics such as infrastructure, health outcomes and economic indicators, together with resources to analyse and use this data for the community's benefit.

- *Capacity building.* There should be investment in digital capacity in civil society organizations, grassroots groups and underrepresented communities so that they can participate in digital governance as informed actors, not just as subjects of others' decisions.

Sequencing the reforms

The aforementioned reforms are substantial, spanning procurement, talent, governance structures, accountability mechanisms, and the fundamental relationship between institutions and communities. Faced with such a comprehensive agenda, the risk is paralysis or worse, attempting everything at once and achieving nothing. The challenge is to sequence reforms in ways that build momentum, demonstrate value early, and create the political and institutional conditions for deeper change.

Four sequencing principles should guide reform efforts.

1. *Foundations before superstructure.* Governance mechanisms and data infrastructure must precede ambitious AI deployment, because the absence of coordination capacity is the single most common cause of implementation failure in UK digital history.

2. *Proof before scale.* Reforms should begin with two or three high-visibility pilots (this book suggests DWP benefit processing and HMRC compliance analytics), where success can demonstrate value and build political support before wider rollout.

3. *Capability before mandate.* Organizations should not be required to adopt new practices until the skills, tools and institutional support are in place for them to succeed, a lesson drawn directly from the GDS experience analysed in chapter 2.

4. *Design for political survival.* Any multiyear reform programme will span at least one election.

Reforms that embed themselves in institutional structures, build cross-party coalitions and deliver measurable citizen-facing benefits are far harder for successor governments to reverse than those that exist primarily as strategy documents.

To deliver on this, chapter 8 sets out a detailed implementation road map, phased across five years, with specific targets for governance, procurement, infrastructure and skills at each stage. This timeline applies these principles to the institutional reforms proposed in this chapter. However, to understand and contextualize what adaptive institutions require, subsequent chapters explore several of the highest priority themes.

Conclusions: from fragmentation to adaptive coherence

The UK's current approach to digital transformation and AI governance is characterized by fragmentation: different government departments pursuing different strategies, different sectors following different practices, civil society outside the tent rather than inside it and affected communities having a voice but limited power. The result is that individual initiatives may be excellent, but they do not add up to systemic transformation.

The blueprint outlined in this chapter points toward something different. It advocates adaptive institutions operating in coherent ways, with shared principles guiding action, inclusion built in from the start and learning systems ensuring that the system continuously improves. This is not a utopian vision. Elements already exist in pockets across the UK. The task is to connect these elements, resource them adequately and make adaptive governance systemic rather than exceptional.

The remaining chapters in this part of the book explore how to build the foundations for adaptive institutions via the skills and capabilities people need (chapter 5), and the ethical frameworks that must guide practice (chapter 6).

CHAPTER 5

Building the UK's AI workforce

Redesigned institutions require redesigned capabilities. The foundation for any lasting AI transformation is social and human: the talent, skills, learning capacity and inclusive participation of people across the UK.

This chapter shifts the focus from institutional architecture to social fabric. It examines how skills systems, talent development and the health of learning culture are not ancillary concerns but the essential foundation on which sustainable digital transformation must rest.

Introduction: reframing skills, talent and inclusion in the age of AI

It is tempting to view digital transformation as primarily a technological or economic story about platforms, algorithms, competitiveness and productivity. But as the UK's experience over the past two decades repeatedly demonstrates, the true foundation of transformation is social, not technical. The capacity of a country to adapt is defined, above all, by the depth and breadth of its talent, the inclusiveness of its skills systems and the health of its learning culture.

The current debate around AI amplifies longstanding challenges. The speed and scale of digital innovation have outpaced the ability of public institutions, private firms and wider society to keep up. Workforce surveys, employer interviews and policy reports describe a world wrestling with skills mismatches, digital divides, and a growing disconnect between education systems and labour market reality. While headline statistics focus on coding certificates, STEM graduates or AI PhDs, they rarely tell the full story of practical digital literacy, interdisciplinary thinking, ethical adaptation, and the skills of collaboration, creativity, critical reasoning and resilience that underpin successful transformation.

Historical roots

The roots of this crisis are deep. Early digital modernization efforts in government, from the 2000s onwards, regularly underestimated the challenge of retraining large, dispersed civil service workforces.[1] As GDS case studies reveal,[2] success was often a function of building inclusive, practitioner-driven learning communities rather than simply importing digital talent from the private sector. In healthcare, the NHS's journey to digital similarly spotlighted the centrality of workforce engagement:[3] national upgrades faltered when front line staff felt left out; progress surged where local digital nurse networks, practice-sharing forums and funded skills development took root.[4] Outside government, the creative industries led some of the UK's most inventive skills experiments, blending informal mentorship, peer exchange and boundary-crossing professional development into new forms of collective learning.[5]

Against this background, successive governments launched digital skills 'grand challenges', STEM expansion plans, coding curricula and talent accelerators. These provided much-needed investment and visibility, but too often defaulted to narrow measures of success – graduate numbers, short-term job placements, high-profile competitions – rather than the sustained development of broad-based, adaptive learning cultures.

The current picture

These failings remain unresolved. At one end, according to recent Office for National Statistics[6] and Nesta[7] surveys, nearly ten million adults in the UK lack the essential digital skills for modern employment and everyday civic life, a group that includes significant numbers of young adults, rural workers and those most exposed to economic churn. At the other end, the tech sector, finance industry and government digital programmes report chronic shortfalls of advanced AI and data science talent,[8] with long vacancies, spiralling salary inflation and heavy reliance on global recruitment despite considerable investment in STEM higher education.

Policy interventions have sought to bridge these divides. The 'Digital Skills for the UK Economy' white paper,[9] the AI Council Roadmap, and the Department for Culture, Media and Sport sector deals have invested capital and strategic energy in education and employer upskilling. The results are patchy. A 2024 National Centre for Computing Education audit found significant North–South divides, the underrepresentation of girls and minority ethnic students, and a large proportion of schools lacking foundational technical teaching capability.[10] The pipeline from tertiary education into industry, especially for AI-specific roles, suffers from disconnection, with few graduates entering directly and many lacking the practical experience employers require.

The digital divide compounds these policy shortcomings. Regional investment in skills infrastructure lags behind London, Cambridge and selected tech clusters. Ethnic minorities, women and older adults are structurally disadvantaged by credentialing practices, access to training and a lack of targeted support. The underlying problem is not simply lack of internet access or devices: it is low trust, weak confidence and thin affiliation with learning communities.[11] The Covid-19 pandemic's forced digital pivot temporarily accelerated adoption, but subsequent research shows that these gains were unevenly distributed and, without deliberate reinforcement, largely temporary.[12]

The case for systemic renewal

The urgency now is not simply to close the gap between what the economy demands and what education offers. It is to rethink learning itself: to move from static, front-loaded approaches where formal education prepares for a single career to lifelong pathways that integrate formal instruction, informal peer mentoring, workplace innovation and personal adaptation. As the pace of AI development accelerates, no single qualification or training programme will suffice. What matters is the system's overall capacity to grow, connect and renew its capabilities.

AI is fundamentally disrupting the mechanics of learning, shifting the focus from the acquisition of knowledge to the navigation of it. Traditional 'just-in-case' education that involves stockpiling information for future use gives way to 'just-in-time' learning, where AI tools provide immediate, personalized feedback within the flow of work. The priority shifts from managing fixed expertise to orchestrating a culture of continuous, technology-enabled adaptation.

This shift means addressing questions of access and inclusion head on. The UK will not unlock digital advantage if entire regions, sectors or communities are left behind. The lessons from digital government pilots, health workforce experiments and creative innovation hubs all underline the same reality: learning is collective, iterative and profoundly social. The sectoral evidence that follows shows what this looks like in practice and where it breaks down.

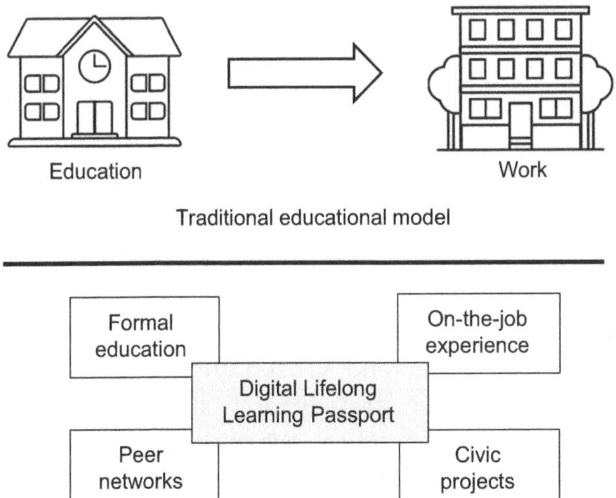

Figure 4. A new social contract for learning.

What works: lessons from four sectors

NHS and public sector: practice-based learning and workforce adaptation

Within the NHS, digital transformation has unfolded in waves, shaped as much by front line realities as by ministerial directives. Early centralization efforts met resistance when staff felt excluded from both planning and skill renewal. The second wave of NHS digital transformation involved nurse-led digital champions, local skill-sharing workshops and participatory networks across trusts.

One notable initiative, the Digital Nurse Network, created a forum where nurses and allied practitioners exchanged learning, shared frustrations, and collectively iterated digital protocols for triage and recordkeeping.[13] Policy documents praised the rapid rollout of e-referral and AI-assisted diagnostics, but on the ground, progress depended on daily collaboration, peer mentoring and constructive 'failure stories'.[14]

A regional digital pilot in Manchester, for example, addressed burnout and skills gaps by embedding digital mentors into clinical teams, running frequent scenario sessions and organizing peer-to-peer feedback events. Implementation surveys showed higher digital confidence, quicker adoption of new tools and reductions in resistance to change.

Similar lessons played out in local government. Work with council digital teams and cross-authority practice groups showed that top-down strategy rarely sticks unless reinforced by communities of practice. When digital apprenticeships expanded, success was mapped not only to technical knowledge, but to trust, resilience, and the ability to experiment and learn together.

Finance and fintech: bootcamps, mobility and talent clusters

In the UK's financial services sector, skills have become a critical currency, superseding traditional job structures as firms transition into skills-based organizations. According to a recent UK survey,[15] while 75% of firms are already utilizing AI, adoption is currently hampered not just by a lack of specialist talent, but by a significant deficiency in managerial guidance and few clear use cases for the existing workforce. To counter this, leading firms are embedding skills strategies directly into business strategy, with over half of boards now discussing skills needs at least quarterly.

A focus on career mobility has become a priority for many financial services organizations, with aggressive reskilling programmes to transition front line and mid-career staff into high-demand technical paths such as software and data engineering. To ensure employees have time for this future-focused development, firms are actively reducing mandatory learning hours (in some cases by more than 60%) and shifting their focus toward measuring 'active learners' who consistently engage in non-mandatory, self-directed growth.

Despite these gains, the sector still maintains the highest share of in-demand roles in the UK, with data analyst, software engineer and digital technology positions remaining notoriously hard to fill. To bridge this gap, the industry is leading the way in skills-based hiring, increasingly removing traditional degree requirements to access a broader, more diverse talent pool.

Creative industries: informal learning, peer networks and social capital

The UK's creative industries have emerged as digital skills leaders, not through formal institutional channels, but via grassroots innovation. In music tech, gaming, interactive design and digital arts, networked learning communities and peer-to-peer mentor schemes account for much of the sector's adaptive capacity. Freelancers and microenterprises form informal clusters, host co-design workshops and run skills exchanges, creating flexible models of professional growth.[16]

Qualitative research and workshop findings from creative clusters in Manchester, Glasgow and Bristol reveal the importance of trust, openness and recognition in skill-building.[17] Where institutional educational models lag, creative networks blend improvisation and social capital. Diverse voices become heard in ways that formal channels seldom support.

However, exclusion persists and access to networks, funding and recognition is uneven. Policy innovation is needed to reward informal learning, validate alternative credentials and overcome the status barriers that block entry for minorities and regional talent.

Government, policy and the sectoral learning divide

Digital government reforms have repeatedly encountered learning obstacles: overstretched budgets, change fatigue and variable institutional readiness.[18] Experience with national reforms underscores the need for visible practitioner leadership, cross-agency networks, and the normalization of iterative failure and corrective learning.

To overcome this, the UK government has launched an intensive upskilling agenda aimed at making 10% of the civil service technical experts by 2030. Central to this effort is the 'One Big Thing' initiative, which in 2025 focused on 'AI for All', providing 470,000 civil servants with foundational training to use AI safely and responsibly.[19] This is supported by the 'Get Tech Certified' campaign,[20] which offers free access to more than 200 professional certifications in high-demand fields such as cybersecurity and data engineering. These efforts are underpinned by the Government Digital and Data Capability Framework, which provides a standardized 'Skills A to Z' to help departments identify and bridge technical gaps across the workforce.[21]

These efforts are having an impact. Agencies that invest in local digital leaders, open knowledge platforms, and rotation programs for technical and non-technical staff achieve stronger transformation outcomes.[22] Conversely, those that treat skills as a one-off investment see lower returns, greater resistance and slower change cycles.

Barriers to inclusion

Gender, ethnicity and the missing majority

Despite two decades of diversity pledges, the digital and AI workforce in the UK remains stubbornly unbalanced. Women account for less than 20% of core tech roles, with even lower representation in data science, AI research and digital leadership.[23]

Ethnic minorities and Black professionals are underrepresented at every seniority level, with evidence of significant disparities in recruitment, pay and career stability.[24]

These gaps are not the result of a single barrier but of a tangled web of exclusion, including the following.

- *Stereotypes and early discouragement* in the classroom, where girls and students from minority backgrounds report lower confidence and fewer role models.
- *Gatekeeping through credentialism* by demanding expensive degrees, formal certifications and work histories that systematically filter out candidates who are talented but lack privileged networks.
- *Limited visibility of non-metropolitan talent*: rural, coastal, and 'left behind' regions are rarely represented in major policy, funding or national digital debates.
- *Workplace culture and burnout*: women and minorities face microaggressions, invisible labour and a lack of flexible, supportive environments in many organizations.

Research based on interviews with new entrants and veteran professionals in tech, health and creative fields confirm the costs. Promising candidates drop out, settle for lateral moves or abandon digital work entirely rather than fight persistent structural bias.

Regional and social barriers

The digital divide in the UK is not just urban–rural, but layered by income, geography and institutional affiliation.[25] Case studies from the North East, coastal towns and towns such as Blackpool reveal weak digital infrastructure, patchy access to skills programs and the near absence of major employers or sector anchor firms.[26] Local skills and innovation efforts, when present, are often grassroots and underfunded.

Government levelling-up funds and regional digital academies have made some impact, but policy churn, short-term funding cycles, and highly centralized program design have limited local agency and sustainability. Many local leaders describe feeling marginal to the national debate, unable to influence program design or access aligned mentorship and recruitment networks.

Informal versus formal learning: recognition and reward

A persistent critique running through creative industries, SME clusters and civic innovation spaces is that informal learning (including peer-led networks, on-the-job experimentation and regionally-rooted communities of practice) remains invisible or undervalued compared with university degrees or formal apprenticeships.[27] Diverse, non-metro voices and entry paths are too often ignored by national employers and policymakers. Without methods to recognize and reward real-world skills, valuable talent is lost and local innovation suppressed.

Research from creative sector collaborations, NHS transformation programs and regional innovation hubs stresses that formal and informal learning are not in competition but must be made mutually reinforcing.[28] Only when credentialing is broadened through digital badges, portfolio-based evaluation and peer-led references does the sector gain resilience and plasticity.

Structural inequalities and economic churn

Economic precarity, especially in gig and freelance economies (such as digital content creators, creative technologists, transport workers and carers), increases exclusion.[29] Those without stable income or organizational backing struggle to access professional training, secure placements or fund the periods of transition necessary for upskilling. Digital change is too often experienced by these groups as a threat rather than an opportunity.

Moreover, automation, algorithmic assessment and global platformization accelerate churn. Low- and mid-skill jobs that are both digital and non-digital are exposed to technological displacement without parallel investments in reskilling, counselling or mobility support. Government programs, when they exist, are oversubscribed and processed by outsourced agencies distant from local labour realities.[30]

The critical choice when investing in skills is whether to protect long-term skill development from short-term budget pressures using tools such as dedicated funding or legal commitments, or to keep treating skills spending as optional. The first approach constrains fiscal flexibility when other urgent needs emerge; the second produces the persistent pattern of launching programs with fanfare, funding them modestly for a limited period, then cutting them when pressures mount. Both are defensible depending on whether skills are foundational or simply part of a broader set of organizational improvements. What is indefensible is claiming that skills are critical while funding them as if they are optional.

Risk of inaction

Without deep systemic renewal, the UK is at risk of compounding digital divides and undermining its own ambitious narratives of 'AI for all'. Organizational inertia, overreliance on formal qualifications and exclusion threaten to cement a two-tier workforce: a core of highly mobile, metropolitan talent and a periphery of underresourced, insecure and excluded workers. Such a future brings a range of risks.

- *Economic stagnation.* Failure to address regional and sectoral exclusion translates directly to greater unemployment, stagnating wages and a shrinking tax base, especially outside major cities.

- *Social division.* A digital- and data-literate elite, increasingly cut off from the majority, fuels public distrust, populism and scapegoating of technology. 'Levelling up' becomes a slogan rather than a reality.

- *Innovation bottleneck.* Start-ups, the public sector and SMEs struggle to mobilize skills when expertise, mobility and networks become concentrated in privileged clusters.

- *Civic disempowerment.* AI-enabled decision-making without broad-based digital citizenship erodes collective voice, transparency and accountability in public life.

History shows that 'skills gaps' are not neutral phenomena.[31] Rather, they reinforce existing inequalities, slow adaptation and limit who gets to shape the future.

Reality check: skills investment competes with everything else

The skills challenge is not primarily a design problem: we know what works – sustained funding for lifelong learning, accessible upskilling pathways, flexible credentials, regional delivery infrastructure, equity-focused pipelines. The evidence is clear. What is missing is not understanding but political willingness to prioritize multiyear skills investment when it competes with every other budgetary demand.

Skills development shows benefits slowly. A young person starting a digital apprenticeship in 2025 becomes a productive AI practitioner in 2027–8. Regional learning infrastructure launched today influences economic geography in 2030. Equity initiatives funded now shift workforce demographics by 2035. This timeline is incompatible with political cycles measuring success in years, not decades.

The fiscal reality is brutal. Every pound committed to skills development is a pound not spent on healthcare waiting lists, not invested in physical infrastructure, not allocated to immediate crisis response. When budgets tighten, as they inevitably do, skills programs are vulnerable precisely because their benefits are distant and diffuse. Cutting a skills program today creates problems in five years when the same shortages are faced by different politicians. The incentive structure systematically undervalues long-term capability building.

This explains the persistent pattern: launch skills initiatives with fanfare, fund them modestly for two or three years, then reduce or eliminate the funding when budgetary pressures emerge. The cycle repeats, with new programs addressing gaps the previous programs were meant to fix. Organizations learn not to rely on public skills funding because it is unreliable. Individuals hesitate to commit to long learning pathways because support may evaporate mid-course.

Breaking this pattern requires mechanisms that protect long-term skills investment from short-term political pressures. Some nations achieve this through hypothecated taxes, constitutional commitments or independent funding bodies. The UK has chosen none of these approaches. Instead, skills investment remains discretionary spending, vulnerable to each budget cycle.

The uncomfortable question is as follows: if skills are foundational to AI transformation, are leaders willing to create funding mechanisms that survive political cycles? Or will skills remain rhetorically prioritized but fiscally marginalized? The answer will determine whether the UK builds the capabilities its AI ambitions require or continues cycling through underfunded initiatives that document the problem without solving it.

A strategy for skills

The barriers outlined above of structural inequality, credentialing gatekeeping, regional neglect and funding fragility will not yield to incremental adjustments. They require a coordinated strategy that addresses learning infrastructure, inclusion, civic capability, organizational culture and policy resilience. Six interlocking reforms would move the UK from its current patchwork toward a system capable of sustaining AI-era transformation.

Lifelong learning infrastructure

In an AI-driven economy, the half-life of expertise is ever-shrinking. Career trajectories increasingly span multiple disciplines, roles and industries. The UK must move from its twentieth-century model of front-loaded education, where formal learning prepares for a single career, to a system of continuous renewal.

The UK has attempted versions of this before. Individual Learning Accounts (2001) collapsed amid allegations of fraud within two years.[32] The National Retraining Scheme (2019) was quietly abandoned.[33] The Lifelong Learning Entitlement, which was meant to launch in 2025, has been pushed back and focuses on funding access rather than skills portability.[34] Each failed for different reasons, but a common thread is that none solved the demand-side problem: without employer recognition and individual incentive, no skills record is worth maintaining. Any new attempt must learn from these failures rather than repeat them.

A national 'Digital Lifelong Learning Passport' would anchor this shift – but only if designed around the incentive failures that defeated its predecessors. This means ensuring employer co-investment that gives firms a stake in the record's accuracy; government credits that make maintaining the passport financially worthwhile for individuals; and integration with existing platforms (particularly the Lifelong Learning Entitlement infrastructure) rather than building from scratch. The passport would be a portable record tracking formal and informal achievements, incentivized by government credits and employer top-ups, and linked to peer mentorship and project-based assessment as well as conventional qualifications.

But the passport is only the visible layer. Beneath it, the UK needs modular credentialing using stackable microdegrees, peer-endorsed badges and employer-recognized project portfolios so that learning accumulates regardless of where or how it happens. Publicly funded career transition programmes should offer stipends and coaching for mid-career moves, redundancy upskilling and cross-sector rotations, making 'career breaks' for learning standard rather than exceptional.

Critically, this must include investment in open tools and technologies as shared training infrastructure. Public investment in open-source libraries and common tooling can function as a national training ground, enabling students, SMEs and public servants to learn by doing without prohibitive licensing costs or vendor dependency.

Inclusion by design

The skills challenge cannot be solved by central government or the private sector alone. Cross-cutting alliances between employers, education providers, sector bodies and civil society are essential. These must not act as talking shops but as delivery mechanisms with shared accountability.

Three structures would make this concrete.

- Regional digital skills consortia, co-governed by employer coalitions, further education colleges, universities and civic partners, should build networks for learning, mentoring and job transition at the local level.

- National digital skills observatories, aggregating data from all sectors, should map demand, supply, and mobility and feed evidence into joined-up policy.

- Creative sector alliances, blending freelance co-ops and professional associations, should enable peer credentials and community-based networking for minority and rural talent.

Within these structures, inclusion must be built in, not bolted on. Digital and AI talent pipelines should set goals for gender, ethnicity, and geographic representation linked to funding and public reporting. Informal learning from peer networks, job experience, and civic participation must be validated and integrated into national credentialing systems. And support for digital freelancing and gig work, including portable benefits, skills insurance and access to community hubs, should ensure that non-traditional workers are not excluded from the learning infrastructure they need most.

Digital citizenship

Digital literacy is not only about technical knowledge. It is civic and ethical. UK citizens face daily challenges understanding how digital systems affect privacy, security, democracy and online identity. Digital citizenship should be embedded from primary school upwards, and integrated into social studies and ethics across the curriculum. It includes skills for online safety and privacy management, reasoning about algorithmic bias and fairness in decision-making, and the use of tools for civic participation such as citizen juries and open consultation on digital policy.

Experience from Estonia shows the payoff of universal digital literacy: more than 90% of citizens engage safely in digital government, financial services and health platforms, with lower rates of fraud, exclusion and mistrust.[35] The UK has the institutional assets to achieve something comparable, but only if digital citizenship is treated as a core public investment rather than a niche educational add-on.

Organizational culture

Experience from NHS redesign, digital government and creative communities drives home that workforce innovation cannot succeed by technical upskilling alone. Organizational cultures shape attitudes toward learning, openness to critique and comfort with iterative failure. The teams most successful in transformation create space for experimentation, open interaction and cross-boundary collaboration. Visible leadership, authentic user voice and psychological safety are essential.

Adaptive societies support career movement, reskilling and non-linear learning. Policies that penalize risk-taking, discourage portfolio careers or lock talent into silos harm both individuals and institutions. And the digital world is too complex for any one discipline or cohort to navigate alone: encouraging humility, diversity of perspective and community engagement enables faster error detection, richer innovation and broader buy-in for new technologies.

Building for resilience

Long-term skills strategies cannot rely on electoral cycles or transient funding bursts. Three design features would build resilience into the system.

1. *Policy architecture with built-in feedback and course correction.* Monitoring outcomes relentlessly, adapting incentives and sunsetting failing programmes.

2. *Decentralized delivery.* Trusting regional leaders, practitioners and communities to allocate resources, experiment and adjust.

3. *Public reporting and participatory review.* Treating skills data and reform processes as public goods.

All policy should be anchored in ongoing feedback, user voice and local narrative to listen to the people and places most at risk of exclusion before, not after, strategy is formed.

Learning from international models

Several countries offer instructive models. Denmark's Digital Growth Panel[36] links all employer training funding to user voice, regional consultation and ongoing impact assessment. Singapore's SkillsFuture initiative[37] funds every citizen's learning account and incentivizes small firms to offer collective training, formal apprenticeships and lifelong career counselling. Both treat learning as a national asset rather than a cost item in the budget, and both make pluralism, experimentation and user feedback central features of the system rather than afterthoughts. The UK can learn from these examples without importing them wholesale. The key is to learn from the design philosophy, not the specific institutional form.

Paying for it: funding, metrics and scenarios

As we look forward to the maturing of the AI era, three scenarios highlight the scale of the issues at stake.

1. *Elite acceleration.* London, major companies and a handful of university-tied regions pull further ahead; others lag or adapt only fitfully.

2. *Managed pluralism.* Deliberate investment in inclusion, infrastructure and adaptive networks narrows regional and sectoral gaps, creating platforms for broad, recurring upskilling.

3. *Grassroots resurgence.* Local innovation (often despite central policy) becomes the engine for renewal, with new digital co-ops, creative clusters and civic unions rewriting the map of talent.

The UK's future will likely mix all three, but policymaker intention, resource commitment and institutional design will shape which path dominates.

Funding implications and success metrics

These recommendations require fiscal specificity and clear targets if they are to be taken seriously. The government's 2025 'One Big Thing' initiative trained 470,000 civil servants in foundational AI literacy, a commendably extensive programme. But foundational literacy is the floor, not the ceiling. The civil service target of 10% technical experts by 2030 implies creating or converting roughly 50,000 specialist roles. At current market rates for AI/data skills training (£5,000–£15,000 per person for substantive reskilling, depending on entry level and target competency), this implies a training investment of £250 million to £750 million over five years, even before accounting for salary adjustments to retain talent against private sector competition.

This target is deliberately aspirational. Whether the precise figure is 10%, 8% or 7% matters less than committing to a measurable trajectory and the workforce plan required to achieve it. In practice, the majority of growth will need to come from reclassifying and reskilling existing civil servants rather than net new recruitment. This is both because the fiscal headroom for tens of thousands of new posts does not exist and because the institutional knowledge that existing staff bring is precisely what makes internal reskilling more valuable than external hiring. The current Digital, Data and Technology (DDaT) Fast Stream and apprenticeship routes provide the model.[38] The question is whether they can be scaled by an order of magnitude within existing departmental budgets, or whether a central capability fund (perhaps drawn from efficiency savings attributed to AI deployment) is needed to make the numbers work.

Beyond government, the economy-wide challenge is larger. With nearly ten million adults lacking essential digital skills and employer surveys consistently reporting AI talent shortfalls, a serious national skills programme would require investment at the scale of the Spending Review's £2 billion commitment, sustained beyond the current Spending Review period and protected from the cyclical defunding the previous 'Reality check' describes.

This book's own analysis suggests two funding mechanisms worth exploring. First, a dedicated AI skills levy that extends the existing Apprenticeship Levy to include AI/digital reskilling for existing employees, not just apprentices, and allowing smaller firms to draw on levy funds for AI training. Second, a sovereign AI skills endowment that requires that a fixed percentage (e.g. 5%) of all public AI infrastructure investment is ring-fenced

Table 1. Example AI skills targets.

Target	Metric	By when
Civil service AI literacy	100% foundational AI training completed	2027
Civil service technical specialists	10% of civil service in DDaT roles (≈50,000)	2030
Adult digital inclusion	Reduce digitally excluded adults from ~10m to <5m	2030
Regional AI skills distribution	At least 40% of new AI roles outside London/ South East	2030
Gender representation in AI roles	30% women in core AI/data science roles (from <20%)	2030
Skills funding sustainability	Ring-fenced multiyear AI skills budget surviving ≥2 SR cycles	2032

for skills development in the regions where that infrastructure is located, ensuring that AI Growth Zones build human capability alongside physical capacity. Neither mechanism is without difficulty, but both would address the structural mismatch between short-term funding cycles and long-term skills needs that the UK has failed to resolve for two decades.

Consequently, monitoring progress in skills development is essential. Establishing clear targets requires careful consideration, and they should be validated against current baselines. Their value is not precision but accountability: without measurable commitments, skills investment will continue the pattern of 'rhetorically prioritized but fiscally marginalized' that the 'Reality check' describes.

Conclusions: a social contract for learning

The AI-driven transformation underway in the UK will succeed not because of policy alone, nor technical prowess, but through the everyday work of growing, empowering and recognizing human talent in all its forms. The UK's future as an AI-capable nation will be secured in classrooms, clinics, creative studios, manufacturing floors and local councils – in fact, in every space where people learn, share, adapt and shape collective progress.

The reforms outlined in this chapter amount to a new social contract for learning: a commitment, binding across electoral cycles and institutional boundaries, that every person will have access to the learning they need to participate in an AI-shaped economy and society through flexible pathways, radical inclusion, resilient funding and respect for the full range of ways in which people learn and grow.

Moving from aspiration to reality will require political will, organizational humility and deep respect for the real experiences of the UK's workforce. The next chapters situate this vision within the wider agenda for governing AI responsibly and positioning the UK internationally.

CHAPTER 6

Governing the UK's AI risks and ethics

Risk, ethics and social sustainability are not just compliance checkboxes to be treated as afterthoughts, but foundational principles that must guide strategy from the outset. Without this ethical grounding, even well-designed systems risk reproducing existing power imbalances or creating new harms. This chapter addresses the 'guard rails' and 'ethical foundations' that must frame all transformation work.

Introduction: from compliance to legitimacy

Over the last two decades, the UK has positioned itself as a leader in digital innovation, regulatory experimentation and AI research. Yet the risks and ethics of digital transformation have become increasingly central to public debate, professional practice and policy design. The story of digital risk management is not just technical. In practice, it is deeply historical, social and political.

The historical roots of risk and ethics in UK digital policy

The UK's journey began in the early 2000s, when digital government reforms sought to modernize public services for the internet age. Initial enthusiasm quickly collided with complex challenges: mass data integration, privacy concerns, public sector procurement and legacy infrastructures. Scandals such as the NHS data sharing debacle[1] and early failures in digital disability assessments[2] exposed the depth of the risks, including flawed algorithms, incomplete datasets and insufficient oversight, all of which created systemic vulnerability.

Simultaneously, theoretical debate flourished among futurists, technologists and civil servants. White papers, parliamentary commissions and sector reports debated fairness, contestability, transparency and social value as central to digital transformation. For example, the UK government's 2005 report on 'transformational government' redefined digital transformation as a shift towards citizen-centric services, moving the debate from basic IT upgrades to the creation of social value.[3] It argued that technology should be used to improve fairness and transparency by breaking down departmental silos.

By the mid-2010s, digital adoption accelerated, fuelled by advances in AI, machine learning and connectivity.[4] The rapid pace brought new risks as the increasingly complex systems outpaced the ability of regulators to anticipate unintended consequences, while automation displaced some aspects of professional judgement in education, health and welfare. The rise of 'black box' algorithms and remote, cloud-based decision-making further fragmented responsibility, challenging traditional models of governance and accountability.

Ethics as process, not just compliance

As a result of these experiences, risk and ethics in digital transformation evolved from static lists of principles and regulatory requirements to living processes of anticipation, reflection, learning and adaptation. Major frameworks such as the Centre for Data Ethics and Innovation's principles[5] and the EU's General Data Protection Regulation (GDPR)[6] set benchmarks for privacy, transparency and harm minimization. Yet these principles have often been undermined by systemic gaps: fragmented institutional roles, weak enforcement and technology's tendency to outpace legal reform.

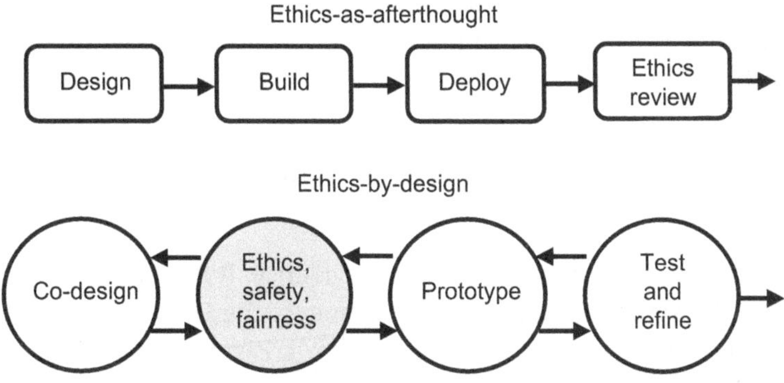

Figure 5. From ethical add-on to 'ethics-by-design'.

Dialogue between public, private and civil society actors has deepened.[7] Civil society advocacy, especially by groups representing the digitally excluded, minority populations and vulnerable users, has elevated the stakes of digital risk. In addition, public backlash over controversial uses of personal data, predictive algorithms in policing and AI-driven grading scandals in education has made ethical governance a core public priority. The challenge is ongoing: how can technology's promise of efficiency, quality and access be secured while respecting foundational values of equity, justice and human agency?

The scope and methods of this chapter

This chapter explores the full spectrum of risk and ethics in AI and digital transformation, drawing on sectoral case studies, comparative international models, stakeholder interviews and critical theoretical debates. It aims to provide the analytic tools for organizations, policymakers and practitioners to navigate (and, ultimately, reshape) the ethical landscape of UK digital society.

The sections that follow provide deep dives into sector-specific risk phenomena (such as the NHS, finance, policing and creative industries), detailed analyses of regulatory frameworks and implementation challenges, extended scenarios of future dilemmas, and practical blueprints for sustainable, participatory ethical innovation.

The legitimacy deficit: the UK's most documented AI failure mode

Before examining sector-specific evidence, it is worth identifying the structural pattern that connects the UK's most significant AI failures. The exam algorithm crisis, Universal Credit's digital hardship and the care.data controversy are typically discussed as separate failures with separate causes. But they share a structural feature that any AI strategy must confront: in each case, a system that *calculated* replaced a process that *judged*, and public trust collapsed not because the calculation was necessarily wrong, but because it was perceived to be illegitimate.

When a teacher assesses a student's grade, they exercise judgement informed by knowledge of that student's circumstances, potential and trajectory. When an algorithm assigns a grade based on a school's historical performance distribution, it performs a calculation that may be statistically defensible but lacks the legitimacy that comes from human accountability. The student cannot ask the algorithm why. They cannot appeal to its sense of fairness. They cannot look it in the eye. This is what Joseph Weizenbaum foresaw when he warned of the consequences of replacing 'judgement' with 'calculation' in domains where legitimacy depends on the exercise of human responsibility.[8]

Universal Credit, as explored in chapter 2, illustrates the same dynamic: automated assessment of subsistence income was experienced by claimants as a withdrawal of human recognition. This is a legitimacy failure, not merely a technical one. And it explains why patients reacted with such alarm to the care.data proposals: the issue was not merely data privacy, but the sense that decisions about their health data were being made by systems whose logic they could not inspect and whose accountability was unclear.

For UK AI strategy, this pattern constitutes a 'legitimacy deficit'. That is, a predictable erosion of public trust that occurs when algorithmic systems are deployed in high-stakes domains without adequate mechanisms for human accountability, meaningful explanation and clear redress. The risk is not hypothetical. It is the UK's most documented AI failure mode.[9] Every AI deployment in public services should be assessed against this risk: not only 'Does this system produce accurate outputs?' but 'Will the people affected by this system experience it as legitimate?'.

The case studies that follow test this diagnosis across five sectors.

Evidence from five sectors

The legitimacy deficit manifests differently across institutional contexts. Five sectors illustrate the range of risks and the variety of responses.

NHS and public health

Healthcare has long been at the forefront of the UK's digital transformation agenda, with the NHS pioneering the adoption of advanced analytics, machine learning diagnostics and patient-facing digital platforms. The stakes are uniquely high: the consequences of algorithmic error, data breach or systemic bias can be immediate and severe, with life-changing impacts for individuals and communities.

Algorithmic risk and decision-making

Machine learning tools are now widely used for triage, diagnosis, predictive analytics and even patient outreach. Projects such as NHS Pathways[10] and AI-driven diagnostics for cancer and rare diseases[11] have demonstrated improvements in speed, accuracy and efficiency when designed and implemented with care.

However, evidence from NHS trusts reveals acute risks.[12] During early pilot deployments, challenges have included calibration errors that led to missed diagnoses and false positives, especially among minority populations whose health data was underrepresented. In one region, a rollout of predictive analytics for emergency room visits revealed systematic bias against older adults, prompting a hasty withdrawal and months of manual review. Furthermore, health professionals have reported feeling pressured to trust systems whose inner workings were opaque yet were themselves held responsible for the outcomes, creating a dual challenge of accountability and professional confidence.

Data governance and patient trust

Experiences from the care.data initiative and later Google DeepMind partnerships offer rich lessons in risk and trust.[13] The push for comprehensive data integration clashed with patient expectations of privacy, transparency and agency. Patient advocacy groups raised alarms over unclear consent procedures, lack of public engagement and insufficient independent oversight. The resulting controversy led to legal action, policy reversals and a mandate for more rigorous audits, engagement and governance.

Ethical dilemmas on the front lines

Clinicians interviewed across NHS digital transformation sites described recurring ethical tensions:[14]

- balancing the rapid adoption of promising new diagnostic tools with the duty to review, challenge and adapt systems in light of emerging problems;

- navigating the intersection of policy mandates, technology procurement and local adaptation, often without clarity about who holds final responsibility; and

- responding to workforce concerns about deskilling, algorithmic authority and the loss of 'artisanal' judgement, especially in cases where clinical nuance and contextual experience matter most.

Sustainable strategies

In practice, the most successful NHS digital initiatives have invested in iterative pilot programmes, routine stakeholder engagement and ethics panels including patients, nurses, clinicians and external experts. Local practice-sharing forums and open review cycles have prevented risks from accumulating unchallenged, allowing errors to be caught and resolved before they cascade.

Collaboration with academic partners has helped trusts develop responsible innovation toolkits for stress-testing for bias, conducting real-time audits and embedding inclusive design. The national frameworks have been informed by the lessons learned, but they continue to depend on there being sufficient resources, active user voice and transparent reviews.

Looking forward

UK Healthcare's experience demonstrates the necessity of embedding risk and ethics not only in central strategy but in front line practice. Participatory reviews, patient-centred design and local adaptation are indispensable for building lasting public trust in AI and digital transformation.

Finance and financial technology

The UK's financial sector, anchored by London but woven throughout the nation, has experienced rapid disruption from AI and data-driven systems. Algorithmic trading, digital onboarding, robotic process automation and personalized financial services are now industry norms. As finance and tech have converged, sectoral regulators and institutions have navigated significant opportunities and risks.

Algorithmic trading and market integrity

The introduction of high-frequency trading and complex algorithmic decision-making has increased market liquidity and enabled new product innovations. Yet it has also engineered new forms of systemic fragility. 'Flash crashes', as experienced in sudden, algorithm-driven sell-offs, have occurred on major exchanges, revealing how interconnected algorithms can transmit errors almost instantaneously.[15] In one case, a trading algorithm's flawed risk parameter, missed by review, propagated multimillion-pound market losses in minutes, forcing trading halts and triggering regulatory oversight.[16]

Bias and risk in retail banking

AI systems are now used widely to automate lending decisions, underwrite insurance and identify fraudulent transactions. While these processes allow for efficiency gains, interviews with sector professionals highlight sources of algorithmic risk: biases in underwriting data, incomplete historic records or insufficiently stress-tested models can result in discriminatory outcomes.

For example, a 2023 review of UK retail banking found that automated credit scoring systems denied loans disproportionately to applicants from minority communities and low-income postcodes, despite no increase in actual default risk.[17] Activists and financial ombudsmen intervened, pressing for open audits, justifications and 'human-in-the-loop' protections for customers.

Compliance, regulation and ethics

The FCA has pioneered regulatory sandboxes consisting of controlled environments for testing new digital products.[18] They are intended to advance innovation while managing consumer and systemic risk. However, this approach is double-edged: while some fintech start-ups proactively invest in external audits and ethics reviews to build trust, others see sandboxes as a license to outpace regulators, deploying products faster than risks can be fully assessed.

Public crises, including major data breaches and high-profile algorithmic errors, have spurred new guidance, audit requirements and whistleblower frameworks. Yet interviews with compliance officers and AI developers indicate that ethical implementation still depends on professional culture, organizational resources and the willingness of leadership to prioritize transparency over short-term gain.

Resilience through alliances and learning

Some of the sector's most promising reforms have involved cross-institutional alliances: skill-sharing across firms, open reporting of incidents and the development of sector-wide 'playbooks' for responsible innovation. Professional bodies increasingly support ongoing education for staff in data ethics, bias mitigation and responsible design.[19] This suggests that resilience and adaptability must become sectoral, not just organizational, attributes.

Policing and justice

Policing and justice have become prominent battlegrounds in the debate over digital ethics and risk. The use of predictive models that algorithmically generate risk scores for recidivism, hotspot policing and resource allocation has been piloted in several UK forces.[20] These tools promise more objective, data-driven interventions, but they have frequently run into controversy.

Civil rights groups and independent audits have uncovered troubling patterns: the training data used for these systems often contained historical bias, overpolicing of minority communities and incomplete reporting.[21] As a result, the models amplified pre-existing inequalities, leading to disproportionate deployment of police resources in certain neighbourhoods.

A national review of facial recognition technologies found significant disparities in accuracy (for example, misidentifying minority individuals at much higher rates than white subjects). Public engagement with these findings was intense: protests, parliamentary inquiries, and legal challenges forced greater transparency as well as a re-evaluation of deployment standards.

Accountability and contestability

More broadly, justice sector professionals have expressed concern over the 'black box' nature of many AI-based systems.[22] Judges, legal advocates and police officers often lacked access to the underlying logic of risk, making it difficult to contest or justify algorithmic recommendations. In one documented case, a defendant was denied bail based in part on an algorithmic risk assessment. Only through expert review was it revealed that the system's logic was flawed, leading to a reversal.[23]

Efforts to improve transparency include the publication of system documentation, routine external audits and the adoption of contestability mechanisms. All with the goal of enabling individuals to challenge algorithmic decisions. While progress has been made, implementation remains uneven, and advocacy groups continue to press for stronger oversight and user representation.

Training and cultural change

One positive development has been the establishment of ethics training and multidisciplinary oversight panels in several police authorities. Community engagement initiatives, user panels and cross-sector learning have helped align system development with broader societal values. However, tensions persist between efficiency-driven reforms and the imperative for justice, due process and the recognition of systemic bias.

Education

In education, risk and ethics debates exploded into the national conversation during the A-level algorithm crisis of 2020.[24] A system intended to deliver fair exam outcomes in the absence of in-person assessments ended up penalizing students from state schools, disadvantaged backgrounds and minority communities. The episode triggered widespread public protest, parliamentary debate and a reversal of policy. It is a powerful example of the social impact of algorithmic opacity and rushed deployment.

Beyond exams, AI-powered tools are increasingly used for admissions, targeted interventions and personalized learning. Researchers and advocacy groups have raised concerns about bias in recommendation and assessment models, the risks of data privacy breaches, and the lack of redress if decisions are incorrect or unfair.

Teacher experience and student agency

With respect to Generative AI, recent feedback from teachers and other education professionals has revealed mixed experiences:[25] while AI-enabled platforms supported differentiated instruction and helped identify struggling students, educators and administrators also felt pressure to rely on opaque systems in ways that diminished professional agency. Student groups, especially those from underrepresented backgrounds, worried that digital interventions could entrench disadvantage rather than mitigate it unless robust oversight and active feedback mechanisms were in place.

Government reviews have led to new recommendations,[26] including transparency in model development, channels for challenge and appeal, and investment in data literacy for educators and students alike.

UK policy and the regulatory environment

The UK has developed one of the most extensive digital and AI governance ecosystems worldwide. The landscape includes the Centre for Data Ethics and Innovation, the ICO, the FCA and Ofcom, alongside sectoral bodies and cross-departmental groups. Parliament has convened several select committees and all-party groups focusing on AI, data and ethics, each producing major reports and recommendations.

Legislation and regulatory guidance reflect an evolving response to both opportunity and risk. The Data Protection Act 2018[27] gave effect to the EU's GDPR,[28] while the 2023 AI regulation white paper[29] set out core goals for responsible technology development and use in the national context. The ICO has led on data stewardship, privacy impact assessment and the development of data ethics toolkits, while the FCA's regulatory sandbox offers controlled spaces for innovation and risk management.

Open and closed models

Open and closed foundation models pose different challenges for UK risk and ethics governance. Closed, proprietary systems allow regulators to deal with a single, clearly accountable provider, but they make it harder for independent experts or affected communities to inspect how models work, replicate findings or test for bias. Open models, by contrast, support scrutiny, research and adaptation (including by regulators and civil society), but they diffuse responsibility across many actors and can lower the barriers for malicious use.

For UK regulators and institutional leaders, the task is not to pick a winner but to tailor obligations to each end of the spectrum. Highly closed models used in high-risk contexts may need stronger requirements for documentation, third-party audits and red-team access as a condition of deployment. Open or partially open models may require clearer expectations about release practices, safety evaluations before weights are widely shared and support for shared tooling that allows smaller actors to use them responsibly.

Across both, common principles still apply: transparency about purpose and limits, channels for contestability and redress, and clear lines of accountability when harms occur. The UK's principles-based approach gives flexibility to adapt these measures as models evolve, but only if regulators have the technical capacity and institutional backing to engage with both open and closed ecosystems on equal terms.

Effectiveness and gaps

Despite progress, critical challenges persist.

- Overlapping and sometimes conflicting mandates across agencies can create uncertainty and regulatory arbitrage.
- Enforcement capacity varies; while the ICO and FCA have the remit and expertise to investigate and sanction breaches, other bodies struggle with underfunding and skills shortages.
- Many ethical guidelines remain voluntary, with monitoring and learning mechanisms often triggered only by crisis or high-profile failure.
- The pace of technological change outstrips the ability of institutions to set, revise and enforce rules. This has led to lag in the face of new AI models, platforms and data-sharing practices.

Parliamentary debates frequently return to these issues: the need for joined-up regulation, sectoral harmonization, more participatory policy development and direct user voice in reform.

Of course, regulation in the UK is not only a question of principles and mandates; it is also a question of control. Regulators' ability to enforce safety, transparency and redress increasingly depends on whether they can access, inspect and, if necessary, halt AI systems and datasets that may sit on foreign clouds or rely on proprietary models whose inner workings are opaque. When high-risk services in health, welfare, justice or finance depend on infrastructure and models that UK authorities cannot meaningfully audit without vendor consent, the promise of 'risk-based, proportionate regulation' collides with the reality of limited digital sovereignty.

Recent developments illustrate both progress and constraint. The AI Safety (now Security) Institute has emerged as a world-leading technical body for red-teaming and evaluating advanced models, providing a new evidence base for UK governance. Yet it is not a regulator and does not itself hold statutory powers to compel access or enforce remediation. The government's white paper response reaffirms a principles-based, pro-innovation approach and signals that binding duties on general-purpose AI developers may follow as risks become clearer. For this strategy to succeed, however, regulators will need not only guidance and coordination, but the infrastructure access, audit rights and international agreements that make digital sovereignty real in day-to-day enforcement.

Why standard responses fall short

Two default institutional responses – greater transparency and more ethics frameworks – have become the UK's go-to reactions to AI governance failures. Neither is sufficient.

Trust is not rebuilt with better communications

When algorithmic systems cause harm (such as discriminatory lending, exam grading disasters or benefits administration failures) the institutional response is remarkably predictable: better communications, clearer explanations, public engagement exercises and transparency initiatives. These are necessary but insufficient. They assume trust erosion is a misunderstanding problem when it is actually a power problem.

Trust in digital systems erodes not because citizens misunderstand how they work but because citizens lack power over how they are deployed. When algorithmic decisions affect people's lives by denying credit, determining benefits or assessing risk, and if those affected cannot meaningfully challenge those decisions, question the training data or influence system design, then mistrust is the rational response. Adding clearer explanations does not address the fundamental issue.

This is why transparency initiatives often disappoint. Publishing algorithmic methodologies satisfies accountability theatre without changing power dynamics. Citizens can read about how the algorithm works but cannot initiate changes when it harms them. They can file complaints that are noted but not necessarily acted on. They can participate in consultations where their input is welcomed but does not necessarily have an impact.

Rebuilding trust requires redistributing power. It means giving affected communities veto authority over deployments that significantly impact them, not just a consultative voice. It means establishing independent oversight with the power to pause or modify systems, not just to observe and make recommendations. It means creating contestability mechanisms where individuals can meaningfully challenge algorithmic decisions and compel human review, not just appeal to the same institution that deployed the system.

The uncomfortable question for UK leaders is as follows: are organizations willing to cede the control necessary to rebuild trust? Or will trust-building remain communication exercises that address symptoms while leaving power structures unchanged? The pattern of the past two decades suggests the latter. Each algorithmic scandal produces calls for better explanation and engagement. Power remains concentrated. Trust continues to erode. The question is whether leaders recognize this pattern as unsustainable or whether they believe incremental transparency improvements will eventually suffice despite repeated evidence to the contrary.

Ethics cannot be outsourced to frameworks

The proliferation of AI ethics frameworks creates an illusion of progress while deferring the difficult work of making specific, costly choices. Every major organization now has an AI ethics statement. Most sound remarkably similar, expressing the need for fairness, transparency, accountability and human oversight. Yet these principles provide limited practical guidance when they conflict, impose costs or threaten commercial advantage. For instance, when a bank must choose between a highly accurate credit model that cannot explain its decisions and a transparent model that performs worse, which principle prevails? Or, when a police force must decide whether algorithmic risk assessment reduces bias or entrenches it, who makes that call and on what evidence?

The UK's challenge is not developing better ethics frameworks but building institutions capable of making and defending difficult trade-offs under uncertainty. This requires something frameworks cannot provide: the political courage to make decisions that will be contested, the institutional mechanisms to revisit decisions as evidence accumulates and the social processes that give affected communities appropriate power rather than merely a consultative voice. Ethics frameworks matter, but they are starting points for hard conversations, not substitutes for them.

Scenario planning, foresight and future risk dilemmas

Internationally, the UK's principles-based approach sits within a competitive landscape where different governance models are being tested in real time. As explored in detail in chapter 7, the

US has moved toward aggressive deregulation; the EU is implementing (and already simplifying) the world's first comprehensive AI legislation; China is deploying state-directed integration at a scale and speed no democracy has matched; and smaller nations from Estonia to Singapore demonstrate that focused excellence and high public trust can produce world-leading outcomes without either deregulation or comprehensive legislation.

The critical question for UK ethics and governance is whether a principles-based approach, enforced by sectoral regulators with varying levels of technical capability, carries sufficient institutional weight to maintain standards when commercial pressures to weaken them are intense. This is a question the EU's recent experience with AI Act implementation has made imperative.

Foresight approaches in UK digital governance

We live in a time of great uncertainty. This brings many challenges as we consider the future of AI and the risks we face assessing its short- and longer-term impacts. Hence, scenario planning has become an essential part of risk and ethics management in UK digital policy. Ministries, regulators and think tanks routinely employ futures workshops, cross-sector panels and digital sandboxes to test for unintended consequences and map possible trajectories. This diverse, adaptive approach is particularly valuable given the rapid evolution of AI and data technologies.

Expert working groups often structure scenarios across multiple time horizons: immediate operational risks (such as cyber-attacks or algorithmic errors), medium-term disruptions (workforce displacement, sectoral concentration, public backlash) and long-term strategic dilemmas (governance of autonomous systems, digital sovereignty, resilience to 'black swan' events).

Illustrative scenarios

Here is a selection of illustrative scenarios that highlight the breadth of risks and ethical considerations that the UK must consider as it plans for future deployment of AI.

Scenario 1: algorithmic society – efficiency versus equity
By 2030, a majority of UK public services deploy AI decision support for resource allocation, triage and eligibility. While waiting times drop and costs fall, systematic exclusion rises among groups with incomplete digital records or atypical needs. Advocacy groups mobilize, demanding algorithmic audits, new user voice channels and guaranteed 'human fallback' options.

Scenario 2: crisis response – AI in a national emergency
A major health crisis triggers the rapid deployment of yet-untested digital triage and contact tracing systems. Initial gains give way to public concern about data misuse and emergency expansion of state powers. Parliamentary oversight, citizen panels and civil liberties groups race to review and recalibrate systems as risks surface in real time.

Scenario 3: democratic backlash – trust and legitimacy
Failed AI deployments in welfare and policing, combined with insufficient remedial routes, foment populist suspicion and resistance. Regional inequality grows as under-resourced communities struggle with disjointed service provision. Long-term recovery requires extensive new investment in participatory governance and civic digital literacy.

Scenario 4: resilient pluralism – ethics-by-design and adaptive capacity
Learning from earlier failures, UK institutions invest in responsive, scenario-based oversight, open challenge mechanisms and diversified infrastructure. Professional, user and citizen

knowledge coalesce into new models for skill-sharing, rapid redress and iterative innovation. Social sustainability is advanced through strong local coalitions and multilevel transparency.

Scenario 5: sovereignty shock – when foreign clouds fail
By the late 2020s, a majority of high-risk UK public services (including HMRC systems, NHS clinical tools, policing platforms and welfare decision engines) run on a small number of foreign cloud providers. A major outage and cyber incident affecting one of these hyperscalers triggers widespread disruption. Tax systems stall, some hospitals revert to paper and local authorities lose access to essential case-management tools for days. Questions quickly arise about where data is stored, which jurisdiction applies and whether UK regulators have any practical means to access logs, verify the incident response or compel emergency migration.

Summary: challenges for policy and practice

Each scenario highlights trade-offs between efficiency and legitimacy, automation and autonomy, central control and plural stakeholder agency. Building resilience involves the explicit design of challenge–response mechanisms, feedback loops and committed funding streams for long-term stewardship.

Establishing these foresight practices, when combined with robust stakeholder engagement, enables institutions to anticipate, debate and adapt to risk rather than simply react to crises. Open futures thinking is increasingly recognized as a key ingredient in responsible AI and digital transformation.

It is important to acknowledge that not all governance is failing. Several models in the UK demonstrate that effective AI and data governance is achievable when the institutional design is right, even if none is yet operating at the scale or consistency required. Open Banking's governance framework, overseen by an independent implementation entity with a protected mandate, has delivered measurable results precisely because it combines clear authority with genuine delivery capability. The Smart Data programme, coordinated through the Department for Science, Innovation and Technology's Smart Data Council, is extending similar principles across additional sectors with growing sophistication. And the NHS AI exemplars programme, for all its constraints, represents an attempt to test AI deployment within structured governance rather than in the ungoverned spaces where most public sector experimentation currently occurs. These are not finished models. But they demonstrate that the governance architecture proposed in the recommendations that follow has working precedents and that the task is to generalize and strengthen what exists, not to invent from scratch.

Recommendations: building legitimate AI

The sectoral evidence and analytical arguments in this chapter converge on a single conclusion: the UK's most persistent AI governance failures are legitimacy failures, not technical ones. Standard institutional responses of better transparency, more ethics frameworks and additional consultation exercises address symptoms while leaving the underlying power dynamics unchanged. Recommendations that follow from this diagnosis must go further.

Closing the legitimacy gap

Every high-stakes public AI deployment should be subject to a mandatory legitimacy assessment: not only 'does this system produce accurate outputs?' but 'will the people affected by this system experience it as legitimate?'. This is the test this chapter's analysis demands, and it requires three specific mechanisms.

The first is named human accountability for every consequential algorithmic decision. Where an AI system determines access to benefits, credit, healthcare, education or justice, a specific individual (not a committee, not a department) must be publicly identified as accountable for the system's operation and its outcomes. This person must have the authority to override, pause or modify the system and the obligation to explain their decisions to those affected.

The obvious objection is defining what counts as 'consequential'. Every automated benefit calculation? Every NHS triage recommendation? Every fraud detection flag? A workable threshold must distinguish between decisions where AI determines or substantially shapes an outcome affecting an individual's rights, liberty, livelihood or access to essential services (where named accountability should apply), and decisions where AI assists human judgement without determining the outcome (where institutional accountability is sufficient). Defining this threshold should be an early task of the AI Coordination Authority proposed in chapter 4 – informed by the aforementioned legitimacy assessment framework and by consultation with the deploying departments that would bear the operational consequences. The threshold will not be perfect. It will need revision as AI capabilities evolve. But an imperfect threshold that creates accountability for the most consequential decisions is better than no threshold at all, which is what the UK currently has.

The second is meaningful explanation rights. Not algorithmic transparency in the technical sense (i.e. publishing model documentation that specialists can interrogate), but plain-language explanation of why a specific decision was made about a specific individual, delivered in time for that explanation to be useful. The exam algorithm's students, Universal Credit's claimants and care.data's patients were all denied this.

The third is clear redress with defined consequences. Contestability mechanisms must be independent of the deploying institution, resourced to investigate complaints seriously and empowered to compel changes to systems, including suspension, when patterns of harm are established. Appeals processes that route back to the same organization that made the original decision are not redress; they are performance.

In practice, this function needs an institutional home. The most credible option is an expanded ICO, which already has jurisdiction over automated decision-making under UK GDPR and data protection law. Extending the ICO's mandate to cover algorithmic redress for public-sector AI would build on existing institutional capability rather than creating a new body. It would require additional resources (the ICO is already stretched) and possibly new statutory powers to compel system modification or suspension. An alternative is a specialist algorithmic ombudsman within the Parliamentary and Health Service Ombudsman's office, which has the advantage of parliamentary accountability but the disadvantage of starting from scratch. Either route is viable. What is not viable is leaving redress as an abstract requirement without specifying who delivers it – which is the current position.

Redistributing power, not just information

This chapter's trust analysis demonstrates that transparency without power redistribution is 'accountability theatre'. Three reforms would shift the balance, each designed to give affected communities real influence through mechanisms that work within rather than against existing institutional structures.

The first is mandatory community impact assessments for all AI systems with significant public impact, sequenced before procurement decisions are made, not after. The procuring authority must publish the assessment and respond formally to community concerns before awarding a contract, giving reasons where it proceeds despite objections. This is not consultation as currently practised (where input is received, noted and filed). It is a structured process where the authority's reasoning is on the public record and subject to scrutiny. The model is environmental impact assessment, which has successfully embedded community voice in planning decisions without giving any single group an absolute veto over national infrastructure.

The second is funded citizen panels with the power to require the modification of AI deployments in specific localities, operating within defined timescales. Where a panel identifies evidence of disproportionate harm, the deploying institution must either modify the system or publish a detailed justification for proceeding. This creates political and reputational accountability even where the deployment continues. The aim is not to make deployment impossible but to make deployment without true community engagement politically unsustainable.

The third is mandatory pre-deployment engagement that shapes system design from the outset, including affected-party representation (with meaningful influence, not observer status) on the bodies that define requirements and evaluate proposals for high-impact public AI systems. This stops short of giving non-specialists voting rights on commercial procurement panels, which would create legal and operational difficulties. But it ensures that the people most affected by AI systems have a structured, resourced and consequential role in shaping them.

From frameworks to institutional capacity

The UK does not need another ethics toolkit. It needs institutions capable of making and defending difficult trade-offs under uncertainty. This means investing in people and processes rather than documents. This means trained ethics officers embedded in deploying organizations with authority to delay procurement, not just flag concerns. It means ring-fenced deliberation time in every high-stakes AI procurement cycle, so that trade-off analysis is a formal phase of the process rather than a box-ticking exercise conducted under time pressure. And it means public reporting not of principles endorsed but of trade-offs actually made: which competing values were in tension, what was decided, what was sacrificed and what evidence informed the choice.

These recommendations are deliberately more demanding than conventional AI ethics prescriptions. They must be, because two decades of evidence from the NHS to the exam algorithm, from care.data to predictive policing, demonstrate that conventional prescriptions have not worked. The question this chapter's analysis poses is not whether these reforms are difficult, but whether the alternative of continued erosion of public trust in the institutions deploying AI is sustainable.

The cost in deployment speed deserves particular attention. Legitimacy assessment, community impact processes and structured engagement all add time to procurement and deployment cycles. The mechanisms proposed are designed to minimize that cost via structured assessments with defined timescales, citizen panels that operate within procurement cycles rather than extending them and mandatory public responses that can be completed in weeks rather than months. The analogy is environmental impact assessment, which adds a bounded overhead to planning processes and which has become an accepted cost of democratic governance in the built environment. The question is whether the UK is willing to accept a comparable overhead for AI systems that determine people's access to benefits, justice, healthcare and education. The evidence assembled in this chapter suggests that the alternative of deploying first and discovering legitimacy failures after the fact is consistently more expensive. The exam algorithm had to be withdrawn entirely. Universal Credit's digital-by-default design required years of costly remediation. Care.data was abandoned after £8 million of investment. In each case, the cost of retrospective legitimacy repair far exceeded what structured predeployment engagement would have required. Speed that produces systems the public rejects is not speed at all; it is waste and delay.

Conclusions: closing the legitimacy gap

The legitimacy deficit documented in this chapter – the predictable erosion of public trust when algorithmic systems replace human judgement without adequate accountability – is not a future risk. It is the UK's most established pattern of AI failure. Closing this gap requires a new social contract that brings risk, ethics and inclusion to the forefront of innovation. This chapter traced how risk is not simply a technical matter, but a profoundly social challenge shaped by history, governance and everyday realities in sectors from health to finance, justice to the creative industries.

In this environment, ethical commitments cannot remain aspirational or abstract. They must be translated into binding, practised realities through institutional stewardship, participatory governance and durable, adaptive policy frameworks. A digitally just society is sustained by transparency, contestability, recognition of informal and marginalized voices, and investment in the ongoing maintenance and renewal of social, not just technical, infrastructure.

The future will only become more complex. Algorithmic systems will grow in influence, data flows will intensify and new dilemmas will emerge at the intersection of autonomy, efficiency and public trust. But with foresight, humility and learning-centred leadership, the UK can remain at the cutting edge of both responsible innovation and ethical transformation.

The ambition must be not only to avoid harm, but to create an environment where everyone can participate, challenge, benefit and adapt. That is the blueprint for sustainable digital society and the promise that this next era of AI can still fulfill.

As explored in this chapter, workforce capability and ethical governance are essential. However, on their own they are insufficient. How the UK positions these capabilities in a rapidly fragmenting global AI landscape will determine whether they translate into lasting advantage. That is the question Part III addresses.

PART III

WHAT COMES NEXT

CHAPTER 7

Where to focus the UK's global role in AI

The global AI landscape is characterized by intense competition, divergent regulatory philosophies and the emergence of distinct technology ecosystems that increasingly operate in isolation from one another. This chapter examines how different nations are approaching AI development, the formation of technology blocs and standards battles, and the implications for UK strategy in an increasingly fragmented global technology landscape. Understanding these international dynamics is essential for the UK to identify opportunities for collaboration, areas where competitive advantage can be sustained and the strategic choices required to maintain relevance in the global AI economy.

Introduction: the global landscape

The UK stands at a defining moment in its digital history. The question is no longer whether the UK can develop AI capabilities, but rather how it positions itself within an increasingly polarized international landscape where different models of AI governance compete for dominance.

As the UK seeks to position itself as a leader in responsible AI development, it must navigate a complex web of international relationships, from the strategic partnership with the US to the regulatory frameworks of the EU, while monitoring the rapid advances made by China's state-directed AI strategy and the innovation taking place across many smaller nations. Across these models, the balance between open and closed foundation ecosystems is becoming a defining fault-line.

Understanding these models is not an academic exercise. The UK's choice among them (or its ability to forge a distinctive path) will determine not only its competitive position but its capacity to ensure that AI transformation strengthens rather than fractures UK society. The stakes extend beyond economic advantage to fundamental questions about democratic governance, social cohesion and national sovereignty in an age of algorithmic decision-making.

The UK's global strategy must recognize that its influence will come not from raw economic or technological power but from thought leadership, standard-setting and the ability to bridge different approaches. Diplomatically, the UK is uniquely positioned to play a bridging role between the innovation-focused US model and the rights-focused EU approach. The UK's historical relationships, language advantages and regulatory creativity allow us to mediate between different governance philosophies.

The UK is already well positioned and should continue to host annual Global Responsible AI Summits, establishing itself as the natural convening point for international AI governance discussions. Additional steps such as placing technology ambassadors in key embassies would ensure that digital considerations are embedded in all diplomatic engagement. Furthermore, influential channels such as the Commonwealth provide ready-made networks for AI collaboration, particularly with developing nations seeking alternatives to US or Chinese models.

Reality check: leadership requires leading

The UK faces a simple choice: lead by demonstrating that democratic accountability and innovation excellence are complementary, not contradictory, or follow by accepting roles defined by others in the AI ecosystem. The current approach of incremental adjustments, consultation processes and aspirational frameworks is choosing to follow while maintaining the rhetoric of leadership. This is neither dishonest nor unusual; most nations find themselves in similar positions. But it is important to be clear about what is happening.

Leadership in AI does not mean matching Silicon Valley's venture funding or Beijing's state coordination. Those competitions are already decided. UK leadership would mean something different: demonstrating that societies can govern powerful technologies democratically, that innovation can proceed within guardrails designed to protect citizens rather than having ethics retrofitted after harms emerge and that smaller nations can achieve outsized impact through focused excellence rather than comprehensive competition.

But demonstrating this requires actually doing it by building institutions that work differently, making resource commitments that reflect stated priorities and accepting short-term costs for long-term positioning. The question is not whether the UK understands what a distinctive path requires. The question is whether it possesses the political will to walk that path when it diverges from easier alternatives.

Four models for AI leadership

Four distinct models offer lessons – and warnings – for UK strategy. Each demonstrates strengths the UK should learn from and limitations it must avoid.

The innovation-first model: learning from the US

The US approach to AI development represents the purest expression of market-led innovation. Underpinned by vast venture capital resources, a deeply embedded culture of risk-taking and regulatory frameworks that intervene only when harm becomes undeniable, the US has established dominant positions across the AI value chain. From foundational research at institutions such as MIT and Stanford to the global platforms operated by companies such as Google, Microsoft and Meta, US organizations shape how AI is developed, deployed and understood worldwide.

The strengths of this model are formidable. US venture funding in AI exceeds the rest of the world combined, creating network effects that draw the world's best researchers and reinforce the cycle of innovation. The result is that US companies do not merely participate in AI – they define its parameters.

Yet this model also demonstrates significant weaknesses that UK policymakers must carefully consider. The concentration of AI benefits in East and West Coast technology hubs has exacerbated inequality, with Middle America experiencing job displacement without corresponding opportunity. The approach of treating ethics as an afterthought in addressing bias, privacy violations and algorithmic harm only after public outcry has eroded trust. Surveys indicate that only 41% of Americans have confidence in AI companies to act in the public interest.[1] The fragmentation of governance, with fifty states pursuing different regulatory approaches while federal oversight remains minimal, creates confusion for organizations and citizens alike. This has led to US President Donald Trump signing an executive order aimed at blocking states from enforcing their own AI regulations.[2]

The recent alignment of UK investment with US technology companies raises important questions. Can the UK replicate Silicon Valley's ecosystem without its unique combination of venture capital, risk tolerance and cultural acceptance of failure? More fundamentally, should the UK attempt to do so?

Answering such questions is made even more difficult with the dynamic nature of this relationship. The US approach has shifted further since this book's core analysis was drafted. The Trump administration has pursued the most aggressive

AI deregulatory agenda of any major economy. Within days of taking office in January 2025, the Biden-era executive order on safe and trustworthy AI was rescinded.[3] In its place, successive executive orders have framed AI development as a matter of national competitive dominance, explicitly rejecting what the administration terms 'engineered social agendas' in AI systems. By December 2025, a national policy framework sought to preempt state-level AI regulation entirely,[4] conditioning federal grants on states not enacting AI laws that conflict with the administration's pro-innovation stance.

For the UK, this shift has immediate consequences that go beyond regulatory philosophy. The September 2025 Technology Prosperity Deal, signed during Trump's state visit, represented the largest commercial package ever secured during such a visit: more than £38 billion in corporate commitments from Microsoft, Google, Nvidia and others.[5] The deal was presented by both governments as proof of a new 'golden age' of transatlantic technology cooperation. Within three months, its continuation has been brought into doubt – not over technology disputes but over the UK's Digital Services Tax, food safety standards and Online Safety Act provisions, which US officials argued would constrain US AI companies operating in the UK.[6]

The continued uncertainty illuminates a structural tension at the heart of the UK's strategic positioning. The UK seeks to attract US investment (and has succeeded in securing headline commitments of extraordinary scale) while maintaining regulatory autonomy on issues from data protection to online safety to tax policy. The US administration views these as a package, not as separable domains. The deal's explicit conditionality that links technology cooperation to 'substantive progress' on trade barriers means that the UK's ability to set independent AI governance standards is, in practice, subject to negotiation with a partner whose leverage is significantly greater. This book's preface celebrates the scale of cross-Atlantic investment. The subsequent suspension demonstrates that investment commitments and partnership stability are not the same thing, and that the 'adaptive path' this book advocates will be tested not in seminar rooms but in bilateral negotiations where the UK's regulatory independence carries a price tag.

The UK's social contract, with its emphasis on fairness, inclusion and collective provision through institutions such as the NHS, sits uneasily with pure market-led innovation. The Cambridge Analytica scandal, which originated in the UK but reflected US-style data exploitation, demonstrates the reputational and social risks of inadequate governance frameworks.[7]

The rights-first model: understanding the EU approach

The EU has pursued a fundamentally different path to the US, one that treats AI as a societal force requiring democratic oversight rather than a purely technological or economic phenomenon. Through landmark legislation including the GDPR, the AI Act and the Digital Services Act, the EU has constructed the world's first comprehensive legal framework for AI governance. This approach prioritizes fundamental rights, transparency and accountability above rapid deployment or competitive advantage.

The sophistication of the EU model deserves careful study. Rather than blanket regulation, the AI Act creates a risk-based framework where the level of oversight corresponds to potential harm. High-risk applications in areas such as employment, education and law enforcement face stringent requirements for transparency, human oversight and impact assessment. The framework mandates explainability, ensuring citizens can understand and challenge automated decisions that affect them. It establishes clear liability chains, so that when AI systems cause harm, victims have recourse. Perhaps most significantly, it treats AI governance as a matter of democratic legitimacy, requiring public participation in how these powerful technologies shape society.

This approach has achieved notable successes. EU citizens enjoy stronger protections than anywhere else in the world. The 'Brussels effect' means that EU standards influence global practice, as companies find it easier to adopt single high standards than fragment their operations. The emphasis on transparency and accountability has built higher public trust in the EU than in the US or China. The consistency of rules across all EU nations creates a large, stable market for compliant AI solutions.

However, the EU model also reveals significant limitations. Innovation has measurably slowed, with only 13.5% of EU enterprises using AI compared with 16% in the UK and higher rates in the US and China.[8] Furthermore, the compliance burden is expected to be significant.[9] While this may be manageable for large corporations, it can be prohibitive for start-ups and SMEs who lack dedicated legal and compliance teams. The emphasis on comprehensive regulation before deployment means that beneficial applications, particularly in healthcare and education, may be delayed by years. Most concerningly, the EU faces a brain drain as researchers and entrepreneurs relocate to jurisdictions where they can work with fewer constraints.

For the UK, the EU model presents a complex challenge. Post-Brexit, the UK is no longer bound by EU regulations yet cannot escape their influence. UK companies serving EU customers must comply regardless of our domestic framework. UK citizens, aware of EU protections, increasingly demand similar safeguards. The question is not whether to have protective frameworks (there is strong public support for them), but how to implement them in ways that enable rather than constrain beneficial innovation.

The partnership model: lessons from smaller nations

While attention often focuses on the US–EU regulatory divide, some of the most instructive lessons come from smaller nations that have achieved remarkable success through strategic focus and social partnership. Countries such as Estonia, Singapore, Denmark and New Zealand demonstrate that scale is not destiny. Smart strategies, executed with discipline and sustained through political cycles, can achieve world-leading outcomes in specific domains.

Estonia's digital transformation offers perhaps the most comprehensive example. With a population of just 1.3 million, Estonia has built the world's most advanced digital government. Every public service except marriage and divorce can be completed online. The country saves 2% of GDP annually through digital efficiency.[10] Citizens have complete transparency about how their data is used, building trust that enables further innovation. The key insight is that Estonia did not try to excel at everything. It identified digital government as its area of focus and pursued it with unwavering commitment for two decades.

Singapore provides a different but equally instructive model. Rather than pursuing broad AI leadership, Singapore has identified specific sectors where it can achieve global excellence: financial services, urban planning, healthcare and logistics. The government acts as a platform provider, building shared infrastructure that the private sector can leverage. The regulatory approach balances innovation with protection through sandboxes that allow controlled experimentation. Most importantly, Singapore has achieved whole-society buy-in through extensive consultation and visible benefit-sharing.

The Nordic countries of Denmark, Finland, Sweden and Norway demonstrate yet another approach, one built on social partnership and democratic participation. These nations achieve high innovation rates not through deregulation but through trust. Extensive consultation, transparent governance and strong social safety nets mean citizens support experimentation because they trust that benefits will be shared and harms addressed. The Nordic model shows that consensus-building, while slower initially, creates more sustainable transformation because it brings all of society along rather than leaving segments behind.

These smaller nations share several characteristics that transcend their different contexts. They demonstrate strategic focus, identifying two or three areas of excellence rather than trying to compete everywhere. They invest in infrastructure as a public good, providing platforms that enable private innovation while ensuring public benefit. They prioritize trust through radical transparency about how technology is developed and deployed. They measure success not just by economic metrics but by social cohesion and citizen satisfaction. Most importantly, they adapt continuously, treating governance as an iterative process rather than a fixed framework.

For UK strategy, these smaller nations offer lessons that are more specific and more uncomfortable than 'focused excellence works'. Estonia demonstrates that two decades of unwavering commitment to a single strategic priority of digital government produces cumulative advantage that latecomers cannot replicate through announcement-driven policy. The UK has declared AI a strategic priority; whether it can sustain that commitment through multiple spending reviews and at least one change of government remains the defining test. Singapore demonstrates that government-as-platform-provider, building shared infrastructure that the private sector leverages, requires the state to be technically capable. This is a condition the book's skills analysis (chapter 5) suggests the UK does not currently meet at scale. The Nordic model demonstrates that public trust is not a soft asset but a hard prerequisite for AI adoption: citizens who trust that benefits will be shared and harms addressed are citizens who consent to data sharing, algorithmic decision-making and public service redesign. The UK's current trust deficit, documented in chapter 6, is therefore not merely an ethical concern but a competitive disadvantage relative to nations whose social contracts support faster, deeper AI integration.

The integration-first model: understanding China's approach

A discussion of global AI models that omits China's approach in detail is incomplete. China represents neither the US market-led model nor the EU rights-based model nor the focused-excellence approach of smaller nations. It is pursuing something distinct: a state-directed strategy that prioritizes the diffusion of AI across every sector of the economy over the development of any single frontier capability. Understanding this model matters for UK strategy not because the UK would emulate it, but because its consequences shape the competitive environment in which UK choices must be made.

China's 2017 New Generation AI Development Plan set staged goals culminating in global AI leadership by 2030, backed by a target of ¥10 trillion (approximately $1.4 trillion) in AI-related industries.[11] What distinguishes the Chinese approach from Western strategies is the mechanism: rather than relying on venture capital or regulatory frameworks, China deploys a proven industrial policy model via the same playbook that built globally dominant positions in solar panels, batteries and electric vehicles but repurposed for AI. National strategic priorities are set centrally; provincial and municipal governments then compete through local subsidies, compute vouchers, model access programmes and innovation zones. Beijing, Shanghai, Shenzhen and Hangzhou each serve as AI pilot zones testing different approaches, creating a form of policy experimentation at scale that few democracies can replicate.

The 'DeepSeek moment' of January 2025 crystallized what this approach can produce.[12] DeepSeek R1, a reasoning model trained for a reported $6 million (a fraction of the amount spent on comparable Western models), matched or exceeded the performance of systems costing tens or hundreds of times more. The market reaction (e.g. Nvidia lost $600 billion in a single day) reflected a sudden reassessment of the assumption that AI capability requires ever-larger capital expenditure. For the UK,

DeepSeek carries a specific lesson: if compute efficiency can substitute for compute scale, the sovereign compute argument shifts from 'how much capacity do we need?' to 'how effectively can we use what we have?'. This does not eliminate the case for sovereign infrastructure, but it changes the calculus significantly.

Equally significant is China's drive to create its own AI technology stack (chips, software frameworks and models) accelerated by US export controls on advanced semiconductors. This is 'digital sovereignty' pursued with a resource commitment and political will that no Western democracy has matched. SMIC is producing 7nm AI chips domestically; Huawei is building sovereign cloud infrastructure; and Chinese firms now dominate open-weight model releases globally, creating developer ecosystems that extend China's influence well beyond its borders.

For UK policymakers, the Chinese model raises uncomfortable questions. If AI advantage flows increasingly from deployment scale and integration depth rather than from frontier model development, the UK's research excellence may matter less than its institutional capacity to embed AI across public services, manufacturing and professional services, precisely the areas where this book has documented persistent failure. China's approach also complicates the 'third way' argument: the UK cannot position itself between the US and EU models while ignoring a fourth model that is actively reshaping the global AI landscape, exporting governance frameworks through the Belt and Road Initiative, BRICS and the Association of Southeast Asian Nations partnerships, and demonstrating that state direction can produce both innovation and diffusion at scale.

What the UK brings

Before cataloguing the UK's AI assets, it is worth asking an uncomfortable question: does possession of world-class universities, a major financial centre and the NHS make the UK an AI

Table 2. A brief overview of national AI strategies.

Dimension	US (innovation-first)	EU (rights-first)	China (integration-first)	UK 'adaptive path' (proposed)
Regulatory approach	Federal deregulation; pre-emption of state AI laws; industry self-governance	Comprehensive AI Act (now being simplified); risk-based with extensive compliance requirements	State-directed; simultaneous regulation and incentivization; algorithmic content controls	Principles-based sectoral regulation with proposed coordination authority
Innovation model	Venture-funded, proprietary frontier labs; $300bn+ hyperscale capex annually	Public–private investment (InvestAI, €200bn); open research emphasis; AI Gigafactories	State-steered industrial policy; compute vouchers for SMEs; integration over invention	Focused excellence in high-trust systems (NHS, finance, justice); AISI as differentiator
Compute strategy	Private hyperscale dominance; Stargate ($100bn+)	Sovereign cloud initiatives; AI Gigafactories; multistate coordination	Full stack indigenization (SMIC 7nm); domestic cloud expansion despite export controls	Hybrid sovereign core (£2bn, AIRR) + managed hyperscale access with exit provisions
Data governance	Minimal federal regulation; market-driven; anti-'ideological bias' framing	GDPR + AI Act transparency mandates; strong citizen rights; cross-border complexity	State access mandated; citizen data as national asset; content controls embedded	Data trusts with fiduciary obligations (proposed); sector-specific regulator enforcement
AI safety/assurance	CAISI (standards); voluntary industry commitments; Biden-era oversight rescinded	Mandatory conformity assessment for high-risk systems; voluntary GPAI code of practice	Mandatory registration and content-safety checks for public-facing models	AI Security Institute (red-teaming/evaluation); assurance as professional discipline and potential export industry

Table 2. Continued.

Dimension	US (innovation-first)	EU (rights-first)	China (integration-first)	UK 'adaptive path' (proposed)
Skills approach	Market-driven; AI education initiatives; STEM immigration priority	Digital Europe Programme; member-state variation; academic strength	National AI curriculum K-12; mandatory tech adoption training; talent retention via scale	Levy-funded, ring-fenced, regionally distributed (proposed); 'One Big Thing' foundational literacy
International stance	Bilateral 'prosperity deals'; AI dominance as national security imperative	Brussels Effect as soft power; multilateral standards via G7, OECD	Digital Silk Road; BRICS/ ASEAN AI centres; UN governance frameworks; norm export	Bridge between models; AISI partnerships; Commonwealth network; standards diplomacy
Primary risk	Concentrated benefits; eroded trust; regulatory vacuum federally; geopolitical overreach	Innovation drag; regulatory retreat under corporate pressure; brain drain to US	Surveillance infrastructure; export of authoritarian governance norms; opacity of state direction	'Third way becomes no way' – distinctive in theory, conventional in practice; regulatory autonomy traded for investment
2025 stress test	DeepSeek disrupts 'scale is everything' assumption; state pre-emption faces legal challenges	Digital Omnibus delays AI Act; Meta refuses code of practice; CEOs call for pause	Export controls drive indigenization; DeepSeek demonstrates efficiency-first model viability	Tech Prosperity Deal suspended within three months; regulatory autonomy versus investment terms not yet resolved

'superpower'? The temptation to answer yes is strong, and the rhetoric of government strategy documents encourages it. But intellectual honesty requires a harder look.

The UK's entire annual AI investment, including the landmark 2025 announcements, is roughly equivalent to what Silicon Valley alone deploys in a single quarter.[13] The UK produces exceptional AI researchers, but a troubling number of them leave. Between 2020 and 2024, many of the UK's most-cited AI academics moved to US-based labs offering superior compute resources and compensation that UK institutions could not match.[14] Events such as the exam algorithm crisis of 2020 has left what might be called 'scar tissue' in public trust and led to a wariness about algorithmic decision-making that government enthusiasm alone cannot dissolve. And the UK's track record on large-scale digital implementation (from the £12 billion NHS IT collapse to Universal Credit's years of hardship) provides evidence that ambition and capability are not the same thing.

None of this means the UK should retreat from AI leadership. But it does mean that the form of leadership must be aligned with reality. The UK is not, and will not become, an AI superpower in the sense of dominating foundational models, controlling the hardware supply chain or outspending the US and China. It is a strategic middle power – a nation whose competitive advantage lies not in scale but in synthesis: the ability to integrate AI into complex, high-trust systems (such as the NHS, the City of London, the criminal justice system) and to set governance standards that others choose to adopt. Understanding this distinction is essential to everything that follows.

The UK's research excellence is perhaps its greatest asset.[15] The universities of Oxford, Cambridge, Imperial, UCL and Edinburgh consistently rank among the world's top institutions for AI research. The Alan Turing Institute provides a national focal point for collaboration between academia and industry. UK researchers have made foundational contributions to machine learning, from Geoffrey Hinton's work on neural networks to

Demis Hassabis's achievements with DeepMind. This research excellence creates a gravitational pull for global talent and investment, evidenced by the recent commitments to the UK from major US technology companies.

The City of London's position as a global financial centre provides another crucial advantage. UK fintech companies such as Monzo, Revolut and Starling have demonstrated how traditional financial services can be reimagined through technology. The UK's Open Banking initiative, which required banks to share data through secure APIs, pioneered a model now being replicated worldwide. The combination of financial expertise, regulatory sophistication and technological innovation creates unique opportunities for AI applications in areas from fraud detection to algorithmic trading to personalized financial advice.

UK national infrastructure organizations such as the NHS, often cited as a particularly challenging target for digital transformation, represent an extraordinary asset for AI development. Unlike the fragmented healthcare systems of the US or the insurance-based models of continental Europe, the NHS provides unified healthcare to 67 million people. This creates possibilities for AI applications at population scale that exist in few places around the world. From drug discovery to personalized medicine to predictive health interventions, the NHS offers a platform for innovations that could transform global healthcare.

The UK's creative industries, including film, television, music, gaming and publishing, punch far above their weight globally and are increasingly AI-enabled. The current challenge for the UK is to understand how to blend technology with human creativity in ways that enhance rather than replace artistic expression. This expertise becomes increasingly valuable as AI raises fundamental questions about creativity, authorship and cultural expression.

Perhaps most distinctively, the UK has repeatedly demonstrated the ability to innovate in governance and regulation.

The GDS demonstrated that user-centred design could improve the transactional layer of public services, though its model also revealed the risks of separating interface design from policy design, a lesson directly relevant to AI deployment. The FCA's regulatory sandboxes demonstrated how to balance innovation with protection. The UK's principles-based approach to regulation, which sets outcomes rather than prescriptive rules, offers a middle way between US permissiveness and EU prescriptiveness.

Sovereignty: the strategic frame

A discussion on what the UK can learn from the AI strategies of other nations would not be complete without a recognition that deeply embedded in the debate is the issue of digital sovereignty. For a middle power such as the UK, digital sovereignty is not about technological self-sufficiency or building the largest models. It is about maintaining the capacity to set rules, secure critical systems and participate credibly in global standards even when much of the underlying technology is developed elsewhere. In practice, this means combining sovereign infrastructure and data institutions with deep participation in international AI ecosystems, rather than choosing between openness and control.

The UK's opportunity lies in crafting a hybrid model. This would mean, at the least, investing in sovereign compute and resilient infrastructure at home, giving regulators and the AI Security Institute the access and tools to evaluate and stress-test powerful systems; building strong public data institutions that can steward sensitive datasets under UK law; and using these assets to lead in AI assurance, standards and regulatory diplomacy. Properly executed, such a strategy would allow the UK to remain open to global innovation while retaining the capacity to govern AI systems in line with its own democratic values, thus moving from being primarily an AI user to a trusted rule-setter and convenor in an increasingly contested digital world.

The urgency of this positioning is underlined by more critical analyse that argue that AI capabilities differ fundamentally from previous strategic resources: they cannot be stockpiled, every query depends on real-time access to infrastructure controlled by a handful of foreign firms, and even sovereign data centres require continuous model updates from providers and hardware replacements from US-controlled supply chains.[16] For a middle power such as the UK, digital sovereignty is therefore not a problem to be solved once but a condition to be managed continuously. This makes the institutional architecture described in chapter 4 as important as the infrastructure investments themselves.

The adaptive model: five principles

Given these realities, a reasonable conclusion is that the UK should not attempt to replicate any single international model but rather synthesize their strengths while addressing our specific context and values. This synthesis should be guided by clear principles that play to the UK's strengths while acknowledging its constraints.

In many ways, the principles that follow of adaptive capacity, deep trust and authentic inclusion sound like an EU governance framework. Distributed decision-making, transparency in design and affected communities brought into governance could be seen by a Silicon Valley executive as precisely the kind of process overhead that has left the EU trailing in AI capability. The objection deserves a direct answer. The difference between what is proposed here and the EU model is not one of aspiration but of mechanism. The EU embeds its principles in ex ante legislative requirements – compliance frameworks that must be satisfied before deployment can begin. The AI Act's risk classification, conformity assessments and mandatory documentation all operate upstream of deployment.

In contrast, the approach proposed here embeds principles in institutional practice – procurement requirements, professional standards, accountability structures and community engagement processes – that operate during and after deployment rather than before it. Regulatory sandboxes test innovations under supervision rather than prohibiting them until classification is complete. Community impact assessments run in parallel with procurement timescales rather than preceding them. The goal is governance that learns and adapts at the speed of the technology, not governance that front-loads all judgement into a regulatory approval process. Whether this distinction holds in practice, rather than just in theory, is the central test of the UK's adaptive path and the reason the implementation road map in chapter 8 includes explicit evaluation points where the approach can be assessed and, if necessary, corrected.

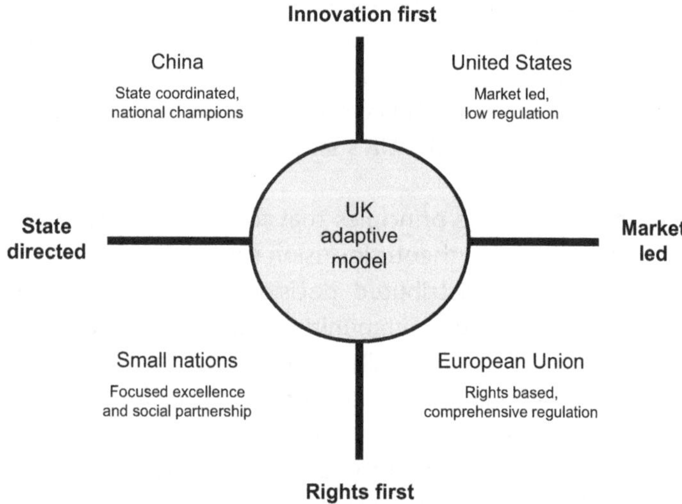

Figure 6. The UK's adaptive model.

The first principle must be ***focused excellence*** rather than universal competition. As seen in smaller nations, the UK cannot and should not try to lead in every aspect of AI development. Instead, it should concentrate resources and ambition in domains where it can have authentic competitive advantage. For example, in financial services AI, the UK can build on London's global position and current fintech innovation to set worldwide standards. In healthcare AI, the NHS provides a unique platform for developing and validating solutions that few other nations can match. In creative AI, the UK's cultural industries' global reach positions it to lead conversations about AI's role in human expression. In responsible AI governance, the UK's regulatory innovation and principles-based approach can establish frameworks that others adopt.

The second principle should be ***trust through transparency*** as competitive advantage rather than compliance burden. The erosion of public confidence in technology companies and AI systems represents both a risk and an opportunity. By making transparency, explainability and accountability central to the UK approach rather than regulatory requirements, the UK can differentiate itself in global markets. Citizens should be able to understand how AI affects them, challenge automated decisions and seek redress when harm occurs. This is not just about protection; it is about building the social license that enables bolder innovation.

The third principle must be ***innovation with safeguards*** built in from the start. The false choice between speed and safety has sidetracked AI governance globally. The UK can demonstrate that responsible innovation is not only possible but advantageous. Regulatory sandboxes allow controlled experimentation. Iterative deployment with continuous monitoring enables quick correction when problems emerge. Ethics by design, embedded from the earliest stages of development, prevents costly retrofitting. This approach requires accepting that some failures will occur but ensuring they happen in controlled conditions where learning is maximized and harm minimized.

The fourth principle addresses the UK's regional challenge directly: ***national strategy with regional delivery.*** AI's benefits cannot concentrate in London without undermining the social cohesion necessary for sustained transformation. Regional AI hubs should be established with specific sectoral focuses that build on local strengths (such as health innovation in Manchester, financial technology in Edinburgh and creative industries in Bristol). Success should be measured not just by total growth but by geographic distribution of opportunity.

The regional choice is whether to concentrate AI investment where existing strengths create the fastest returns (primarily London and the South East), accepting that geographic inequality deepens, or whether to distribute investment to build regional capabilities, knowing that this slows overall growth and requires sustained commitment beyond typical political cycles. The first maximizes near-term economic impact but risks social fracture; the second pursues cohesion at the cost of competitive position. Rhetorical commitments to 'levelling up' are costless; actual resource allocation reveals which goal truly dominates when they conflict.

The fifth principle recognizes that in a world of technological giants, the UK's influence comes through ***partnership rather than dominance***. The UK should lead through collaboration, building public–private partnerships for infrastructure, multistakeholder governance that includes citizen voice, and international leadership on standards and ethics. Where appropriate, we should embrace open source and data sharing, recognizing that our advantage comes from application and governance rather than monopolistic control.

These principles set the strategic direction. Translating them into competitive advantage requires specific, distinctive choices and is explored in detail in the rest of this chapter.

Reality check: the 'third way' risks becoming 'no way'

The UK's rhetoric of a distinctive path between US innovation-first and EU rights-first approaches sounds strategically sophisticated. In practice, it risks becoming an excuse for indecision and a way to avoid the hard choices that defining an appropriate alternative would require. A distinctive path is not simply the average of other approaches or the avoidance of their extremes. It requires distinctive choices backed by distinctive capabilities and distinctive resource commitments.

What would a unique UK approach to AI actually mean in practice? Would it mean requiring data localization for critical systems even if that increases costs and slows deployment? Would it mean publicly funding open-source foundation models as strategic infrastructure even if they lag commercial alternatives initially? Would it mean imposing algorithmic transparency requirements that exceed both US and EU standards?

Without answers to such questions, 'third way' rhetoric becomes empty branding. The UK cannot indefinitely position itself as offering something different while making the same choices as everyone else and pursuing deep integration with US commercial platforms while adopting EU regulatory language. At some point, the UK must decide whether it is willing to pay the costs of establishing distinctiveness or whether its strategy is essentially to be a friendly jurisdiction for others' approaches.

The Technology Prosperity Deal's rapid unravelling, analysed earlier in this chapter, gave this abstract concern concrete form. The 'third way' is being tested in real time. The early results suggest that maintaining a distinctive position requires not just intellectual coherence but institutional resilience sufficient to withstand pressure from partners whose leverage exceeds the UK's own.

Five distinctive UK choices

The adaptive model's five principles – focused excellence, trust as advantage, innovation with safeguards, regional delivery and focused partnerships – find their most concrete expression in five choices that no other nation is currently making. Success for a middle power depends on finding niches – such as critical bottlenecks or unique inputs – that are too difficult for global giants to replicate, thereby turning domestic capabilities into clear international leverage.[17] The five choices below are selected with that test in mind: each represents a capability the UK is distinctively positioned to build and that other nations (including AI superpowers) would have reason to value. If the UK's 'adaptive path' is to mean more than splitting the difference between US and EU approaches, the UK must make specific choices that neither is making. Five possibilities emerge from this book's analysis.

1. *AI assurance as an export industry.* The UK's combination of world-class AI research, a principles-based regulatory tradition and the AI Security Institute creates a unique foundation for becoming the global leader in AI assurance, that is, the testing, auditing and certification of AI systems for safety, fairness and reliability. The institutional infrastructure already exists in embryonic form.[18] The AI Standards Hub (a partnership between the Alan Turing Institute, the British Standards Institution and the National Physical Laboratory) is building capacity for AI standards development. The British Standards Institution's AI committee has published more than forty AI standardization deliverables with more than a hundred in development. The government's 'layered approach' to standards (sector-agnostic, context-specific and sectoral) provides a framework for translating assurance principles into commercially usable specifications. The task is not to build this ecosystem from scratch but to scale and internationalize what already exists. No other nation has this combination of assets. The US approach relies primarily on industry self-governance. The EU approach embeds assurance within a complex legislative compliance framework. The UK could establish AI assurance as a distinct professional discipline and commercial service, with internationally recognized

standards that other nations adopt, much as the City of London established global standards in financial services.

2. *AI in complex, high-trust public systems.* The NHS is the world's largest single-payer health system. If the UK can demonstrate AI deployment that improves outcomes, maintains equity and commands public trust within the NHS, it will have created a replicable model that dozens of countries need. No other nation has a comparable proving ground for AI in complex, high-trust systems. This is a more defensible advantage than competing to train larger language models.

3. *Mandatory algorithmic transparency for public-sector AI.* Neither the US nor the EU currently requires the publication of algorithmic impact assessments for all public-sector AI deployments. The UK could do so, building on existing equalities legislation and the legitimacy deficit analysis in chapter 6. This would mean publishing how AI systems reach decisions affecting citizens, what training data was used, what bias testing was conducted and what redress mechanisms exist. The political cost is that such transparency will reveal imperfection. The strategic value is that it builds precisely the public trust that enables deeper and faster AI adoption.

4. *A 'data trust' model for sensitive public data.* Between the US approach (data primarily governed by private platforms) and the EU approach (data governed by comprehensive regulation), the UK could pioneer an institutional model: independent data trusts with fiduciary obligations to data subjects, authorized to grant access for AI development under transparent, auditable conditions. This would address the legitimate concern that sensitive public data (particularly NHS data) should not be exploited commercially without public benefit, while avoiding the paralysis that occurs when data access is restricted entirely.

5. *Binding infrastructure sovereignty provisions.* As the preface notes, the UK is currently accepting £250 billion in cross-Atlantic AI infrastructure investment. Making 'sovereignty by default' a condition of this investment – contractual provisions for data residency, exit pathways, audit access and regulatory compliance – would demonstrate that openness to investment and insistence on sovereignty are compatible. This is the test case for whether the UK's 'adaptive path' means anything in practice.

Each of these choices involves political cost: transparency reveals imperfection, sovereignty conditions complicate investment negotiations and assurance standards create compliance burdens for UK firms. But each is also the kind of distinctive commitment that prevents 'third way' from becoming 'no way'. A strategy that promises to be distinctive must eventually specify how.

The window for establishing this distinctive position is open but will not remain so indefinitely. Other nations are moving rapidly to establish their AI strategies and capture competitive advantage. The UK must act with urgency while maintaining the patience necessary for sustainable transformation.

Conclusions: choosing the right path

The UK stands at a crossroads that will define its position in the global digital order for decades to come. The billions in US investment, the proximity of EU regulation and the success of focused nations all exert gravitational pull in different directions. Yet the UK's opportunity lies not in choosing sides but in synthesizing these approaches into something distinctively our own.

This synthesis must reflect UK values and traditions: the balance between innovation and equity that has characterized our best moments, the pragmatism that has allowed the UK to adapt to changing circumstances and the global outlook that has defined its role in the world. The UK has always been at its best when it charts its own course rather than following others.

Events since the AI Act's passage have complicated this picture. By late 2025, the European Commission itself was retreating from the framework's ambition. The Digital Omnibus simplification package, published in November 2025, delayed high-risk compliance deadlines, linked implementation to the availability of technical standards that remain unfinished and reduced penalties for mid-sized companies.[19] Meta publicly refused to sign the voluntary code of practice for general-purpose AI, calling the Act 'overreach'.[20] Google signed with explicit reservations that the framework 'risk[s] slowing Europe's development and deployment of AI'.[21] European CEOs, including the head of France's AI champion Mistral, issued an open letter asking Brussels to pause implementation for two years.[22]

This matters for the UK's strategic positioning in two ways. First, the binary framing of 'EU regulates, US innovates' is increasingly outdated. The EU is now engaged in exactly the same negotiation between governance standards and competitive position that this book argues the UK must navigate. Second, the EU's difficulties provide evidence for one of this book's central arguments: that comprehensive ex ante regulation struggles to keep pace with AI's rate of change. But they also provide a cautionary counter-example. The EU's retreat is being driven in part by aggressive industry lobbying from the same US hyperscalers whose investment the UK is courting. If the EU's regulatory ambition can be eroded by corporate pressure, the UK's lighter-touch principles-based approach – which relies on sectoral regulators with less political weight than the European Commission – may prove even more vulnerable. The question for UK policymakers is not whether to regulate like the EU, but whether principles-based regulation has sufficient institutional weight to resist the same commercial pressures that are reshaping EU policy.

The risk of failing to answer that question is brought into sharp focus in Sam Winter-Levy and Anton Leicht's characterization of the UK as pursuing ‘bandwagoning’ by seeking access to a US-based AI ecosystem through ever-closer alignment rather than building real strategic leverage.[23] Whether or not that framing is accepted in full, it serves as a warning: the adaptive path this book advocates must produce concrete, distinctive capabilities that the UK can sustain independently, not merely a rhetorical positioning that collapses at the first diplomatic hurdle, as the Technology Prosperity Deal might.

Success will require courage and bold action. The courage to focus on areas of true strength rather than trying to compete everywhere, to insist that ethical AI is an advantage rather than a constraint and to address the UK’s regional inequalities rather than accepting concentration in London as inevitable. It will require sustained political will, continued investment and the ability to bring the whole of society along with it rather than leaving segments behind. How the UK can succeed on this journey is the subject of the next chapter.

CHAPTER 8

How to deliver the UK's AI strategy

While the UK possesses notable strengths in areas such as research excellence and financial services innovation, converting these advantages into sustainable economic growth requires addressing fundamental barriers including risk-averse investment culture, fragmented governance structures, and the growing divide between AI pioneers and organizations struggling with basic digitalization.

This chapter confronts these challenges directly, examining why previous digital transformation efforts have yielded limited results, the systemic issues that continue to impede progress and the coordinated interventions needed across government, industry and academia.

Introduction: why delivery fails

Strategy without execution is merely aspiration. The UK does not lack AI strategies, white papers or transformation visions. It lacks the institutional capacity to convert them into lasting change. The failures analysed throughout this book, including the NHS National Programme for IT, Universal Credit's digital delivery and the exam algorithm debacle, share a common feature: not flawed strategy but flawed implementation.

Fragmented governance, risk-averse investment culture, and the growing divide between AI pioneers and organizations struggling with basic digitalization are not new diagnoses. They are recurring symptoms of a delivery problem that has persisted across two decades and multiple administrations.

Chapter 2 traced the cycle in detail: early enthusiasm masking complexity, organizational inertia overwhelming good intentions, governance structures designed for oversight becoming barriers to delivery and eventual crisis providing political cover for retreat. The NHS IT programme, Universal Credit and the exam algorithm each followed this pattern with depressing fidelity.

The question for this chapter is not why these failures occurred – that ground has been covered – but what kind of implementation approach could break the cycle. Two insights from the earlier analysis shape everything that follows. First, implementation complexity is not a problem to be solved but a condition to be managed; initiatives that treat delivery as the execution of a fixed plan are already failing, even when early milestones are met. Second, the gap between successful pilot and systemic change is where most UK initiatives die. This is not because the technology fails, but because institutional, political and cultural barriers reassert themselves at scale. The 'design gap' identified in chapter 2, the separation of service design from policy design, explains why technically competent solutions routinely fail to deliver the outcomes they promise.

Breaking this pattern requires foundations that the UK has rarely put in place before attempting transformation at scale, coupled with a clear-eyed understanding of what makes AI implementation distinct from the digital transformations that preceded it.

Principles that work

Two decades of UK digital transformation as exemplified by the work of GDS, Open Banking, the NHS Digital Academy and the

Covid-19 vaccine rollout have produced hard-won implementation wisdom. The principles that follow are derived from those experiences. They are not AI-specific, and that is precisely the point: AI implementation will fail for the same human, institutional and political reasons that have derailed every previous wave, unless leaders apply the lessons already available. Four fundamental principles can be distinguished, each drawn from what the UK has got right, not just what it has got wrong.

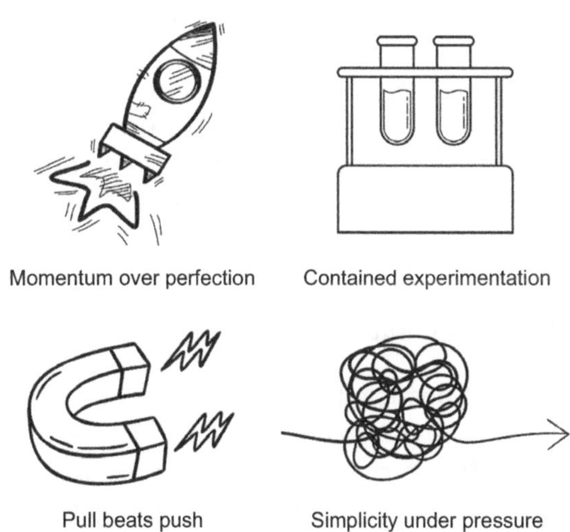

Figure 7. How to deliver: the four implementation imperatives.

Momentum over perfection

Transformation succeeds where enthusiasm exists, not where conditions are ideal. Too many UK implementations fail by seeking perfect pilots in optimal conditions. They overlook the fact that motivated volunteers will push through obstacles that cause forced participants to give up. Successful change begins not with the most important services or the best-resourced departments but with those willing to try something different.

Energy creates momentum, momentum attracts resources and resources enable scale.

This means accepting that implementation in complex environments requires adaptive rather than predictive approaches. Traditional planning assumes that requirements can be known, risks identified and progress scheduled. Digital transformation occurs in environments where none of this holds. Success comes not from better planning but from building the capability to sense and respond to change while recognizing that seeking data perfection is the enemy of progress. Successful implementations build quality incrementally through usage rather than demanding it as a precondition. Working prototypes convince sceptics whom perfect presentations leave unmoved: Open Banking gained support not through policy papers but through working applications that demonstrated real value to real users.

Contained experimentation

Failure is not just possible but necessary for learning. The key is creating spaces where failure can occur without catastrophic consequences. This is seen when running small experiments with a contained impact rather than betting everything on comprehensive transformation. The vaccine rollout succeeded partly because it ran multiple parallel experiments in distribution, allowing rapid identification and scaling of what worked.[1]

But experimentation has a deeper purpose than testing ideas: it builds lasting institutional capability. When transformation is framed as a project with a defined endpoint, organizations unconsciously prepare to revert to previous states. Teams are assembled temporarily, funding is allocated for fixed periods and success is defined as reaching completion rather than establishing new capacity. Sustainable change requires reframing experimentation as capability building and by embedding new ways of working into job descriptions, performance metrics, budget allocations and governance structures so that they persist after the programme ends.

Pull beats push

Mandating change through policy or executive directive typically generates compliance without commitment. Sustainable transformation occurs when people choose to change because they see benefit, not because they are required to. The most successful government digital services are those that civil servants choose to use because they make work easier, not those they are mandated to adopt.

At the heart of this principle lies a focus on the actual experience of users rather than the preferences of stakeholders. Traditional government implementations begin with policy objectives and stakeholder requirements, then attempt to force users to adapt to the resulting systems. Successful implementations invert this hierarchy, making user needs the non-negotiable foundation. And this extends to governance: the shift from asking 'how do we prevent failure?' to 'how do we enable success?' changes everything from meeting structures to decision rights to risk tolerance.

Simplicity under pressure

Every transformation faces moments when stakeholders demand additions, governance requires documentation and edge cases multiply requirements. The instinct is to accommodate, to add and to comprehensively address every concern. But successful implementations maintain almost militant simplicity, defaulting to subtraction rather than addition when pressed. The GOV.UK design principles of 'start with user needs, do less and iterate' were not just design guidance but survival strategies for maintaining focus despite organizational pressure for complexity.

Sustaining what works

The four imperatives get transformation started. Two further practices keep it going. The first is coalition maintenance. The energy and alignment that enable initial transformation naturally dissipate over time: stakeholders achieve their objectives at different rates, early enthusiasm gives way to implementation fatigue and new priorities compete for attention. Sustaining coalitions requires continuous renewal by regularly revisiting the shared vision, ensuring that benefits flow to all participants and not just to early winners and telling a consistent story about transformation that survives changes in leadership.

The second is outcome-focused measurement. Traditional metrics focus on the activity measuring systems deployed, the processes digitized and the people trained. This can create an illusion of progress while missing whether transformation delivers the intended outcomes. Sustainable change requires measuring patient health rather than appointments processed, business growth rather than forms submitted, citizen satisfaction rather than cases closed. Most critically, it means evolving metrics as transformation matures rather than maintaining zombie key performance indicators that have outlived their usefulness.

The critical early period

Momentum in transformation grows incrementally. When gained early, it accelerates progress; lost early, it rarely recovers. The opening period of any implementation establishes patterns, relationships and expectations that persist throughout the journey.

Early momentum comes from visible progress rather than perfect preparation. The temptation is to spend months in planning, requirements gathering and stakeholder consultation before beginning delivery. But action creates energy while planning consumes it. Starting with something tangible, even if imperfect, builds confidence and attracts support in ways that strategies and frameworks cannot.

Establishing credibility through early delivery proves more important than establishing authority through formal structures. Teams that quickly demonstrate competence through tangible results earn the trust and autonomy needed for transformation. Those that begin with lengthy governance discussions and organizational design find themselves trapped in bureaucratic debates before proving their value.

The early period also establishes cultural norms. If initial interactions are hierarchical, that pattern persists. If early decisions require multiple approvals, that expectation becomes embedded. If initial failures result in blame, that fear shapes all subsequent risk-taking. Successful implementations deliberately use their opening weeks to model the behaviours they need: rapid decision-making, user focus, learning from failure and collaborative problem-solving.

The art lies in balancing quick wins that build confidence with foundational work that enables scale. Quick wins without foundations create unsustainable expectations. Foundations without quick wins lose momentum before value emerges. The most successful implementations identify initiatives that achieve both with visible progress that also establishes the capabilities, relationships and patterns needed for broader transformation.

What is different about AI?

The principles in the previous section were derived from two decades of digital transformation. They apply to AI – but AI is not just another digital programme. Three characteristics of AI systems demand specific architectural responses that go beyond general implementation wisdom. First, AI development operates on timescales that resist agile orthodoxy. Second, AI systems behave probabilistically, making evaluation fundamentally harder than testing conventional software. Third,

AI infrastructure raises sovereignty and lock-in questions that conventional digital services rarely confront. Leaders who treat AI implementation as a straightforward extension of the GDS playbook will encounter each of these in ways they are not prepared for.

There is also a structural difference that is fundamental to all three of these characteristics. The GDS playbook assumed that government could consolidate its buying power while diversifying its supplier base. This held true for web technologies built on open-source stacks. For AI, the supply base has reconcentrated into a small number of US and Chinese foundation model providers, making demand-side consolidation not merely useful but essential: without coordinated procurement standards, multi-vendor requirements and interoperability mandates, departments risk accumulating silent lock-in that forecloses future optionality.

The most immediate challenge concerns methodology. The success of agile delivery in UK government was built on a software development paradigm where two-week sprints, rapid iteration and continuous user feedback are natural fits.[2] Some aspects of AI delivery suit this pattern. Many do not. Training a large-scale model can take weeks or months. Evaluating whether a model's outputs are systematically biased may require observing its performance across thousands of decisions over an extended period. 'Correcting' a model's behaviour is not a matter of fixing a line of code but may require retraining with different data, which restarts a lengthy cycle. The implication is not that agile is irrelevant to AI as it remains essential for the service layer. But applying it uniformly across all layers of an AI programme is inappropriate.

AI programmes must therefore manage multiple timescales simultaneously. The user interface, service design and stakeholder engagement can and should follow agile rhythms. The underlying model development requires longer cycles with different governance checkpoints. This is perhaps more akin to pharmaceutical trial phases than to software sprints. And the data infrastructure that feeds both operates on its own timeline, shaped by procurement cycles, data-sharing agreements and regulatory approvals.

Leaders should adopt what might be called a 'nested timescale' architecture: agile sprints for the service layer, structured milestone reviews for model development and long-horizon planning for data infrastructure. Applying a single methodology across all three layers is a recipe for the kind of implementation failure that this book has documented throughout.

Finally, AI implementation demands explicit decisions about sovereignty and openness that conventional digital services rarely force. This means choosing architectures that avoid hard lock-in to a single closed platform, keep options open for sovereign or multicloud deployment, and allow regulators and auditors to see enough of the system to do their jobs. As chapter 7's analysis of the UK's infrastructure choices argued, these are not technical preferences but strategic commitments with long-term consequences for national capability and democratic accountability.

Navigating the risks

Implementation risks are not external threats to be eliminated but inherent characteristics of transformation to be navigated. The UK's experience reveals that certain risks appear with such regularity that they should be considered features of the landscape rather than unexpected obstacles.

Political discontinuity represents perhaps the most predictable yet poorly managed risk. Multiyear transformations inevitably span electoral cycles, yet implementations are rarely designed to address this reality. New governments reflexively abandon their predecessors' initiatives, regardless of merit or progress. The pattern is so consistent that any implementation lasting beyond a single parliamentary term should assume political change as a certainty rather than a risk.

Successful navigations of political change share common characteristics. They embed transformation deeply enough in institutional structures that reversal becomes difficult and expensive. They build broad coalitions that include opposition voices, making the initiative politically neutral rather than partisan. They demonstrate regular, visible benefits that create public expectation of continuation. For instance, it can be argued that initiatives such as the Open Banking transformation survived multiple changes of government because they create value for consumers and businesses that transcended political ideology.

Technical debt presents a different category of challenge, often invisible until it becomes overwhelming. Legacy systems accumulate like geological strata, each layer adding complexity and constraint. The temptation is to declare comprehensive modernization, but such efforts typically collapse under their own ambition. Successful implementations take a more pragmatic approach, wrapping legacy systems with modern interfaces rather than replacing them, creating integration layers that allow gradual transition rather than complete replacement.

The GDS's approach to legacy systems proved instructive. Rather than waiting for departments to modernize their technology, GDS created integration patterns that allowed modern services to interact with legacy systems. This did not eliminate technical debt but made it manageable, allowing transformation to proceed despite imperfect foundations.[3]

Organizational resistance emerges not from malice but from a rational response to threat. Digital transformation can threaten existing power structures, familiar ways of working and established expertise. Treating resistance as a problem to be overcome through force or persuasion typically strengthens it. Successful implementations recognize resistance as information about where change creates real loss and addresses those losses directly.

This might mean creating new roles for those whose current positions are threatened, providing intensive support for those whose expertise needs updating or redesigning changes to preserve valuable aspects of existing practice. For example, the NHS's successful digital initiatives moved forwards precisely because they were led by clinicians who understood and addressed the legitimate concerns of their colleagues rather than by technologists who dismissed them.[4]

Finally, public trust in AI systems represents a unique implementation risk that combines technical, ethical and communication challenges. Trust, once lost, proves extremely difficult to rebuild, as the exam algorithm crisis demonstrated. Building and maintaining trust requires more than good intentions. It requires radical transparency about how systems work, meaningful mechanisms for redress when they fail and appropriate participation in governance decisions.

Reality check: implementation is the strategy

The persistent gap between the UK's strategic ambitions and operational reality reveals an uncomfortable truth: the problem is not that strategies fail during implementation, but that implementation is where strategy actually happens.[5]

What gets implemented, in what sequence, with what resources, under whose accountability – these decisions constitute the real strategy regardless of what policy documents declare. When a government announces ambitious AI transformation plans but then staffs the implementation team with junior analysts on temporary contracts, that is strategic communication about priorities. When procurement rules remain unchanged despite commitments to agile delivery, that communicates which matters more. When ethics reviews can be waived under time pressure, that reveals how principles trade off against convenience.

Over the past two decades the UK has become expert at writing impressive digital strategies. Converting those strategies into the unglamorous, difficult, persistent work of changing how institutions actually operate requires different capabilities: empowered delivery teams, political protection during inevitable stumbles, sustained funding through electoral cycles and willingness to hold leadership accountable for delivery not just announcement. Without this shift, each new digital strategy simply adds to the accumulated pile of eloquent documents describing a future that never quite arrives.

The implementation road map

The principles and imperatives just described provide the foundations for effective delivery. But principles without a plan are aspirations. This section sets out an integrated implementation road map that applies the book's analysis to a concrete five-year programme of reform. It brings together the institutional changes proposed in chapter 4, the skills and ethics foundations from chapters 5 and 6, and the global positioning choices analysed in chapter 7.

The road map is structured in three phases. Each phase identifies specific actions across five delivery strands (governance, procurement, infrastructure, skills and international positioning), alongside the strategic choices and decision points that leaders will face. It is offered as one credible pathway, not a fixed blueprint. The sequencing matters more than the precise dates: foundations must precede scale, proof must precede mandate and every element must be designed to survive political change. Chapter 9 draws together all of the book's recommendations into a single reference framework, organized by theme rather than chapter.

Phase one: laying foundations (2026–7)

The opening phase establishes the essential architecture for everything that follows. The analysis of past modernization

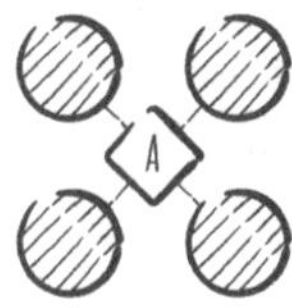

Phase one: laying foundations

- Establish new governance architecture (e.g. National AI Governance Board).
- Launch 3–5 regional AI hubs outside London.
- Develop initial responsible AI certification frameworks.

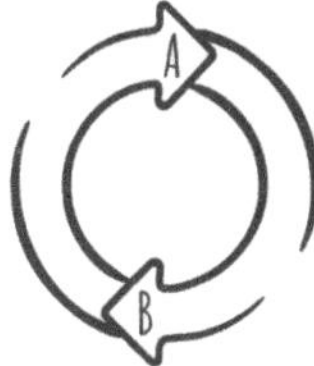

Phase two: building momentum

- Invest in shared national infrastructure (e.g. sovereign compute).
- Evolve adaptive regulations through sectorial sandboxes.
- Deepen international research partnerships.

Phase three: delivering transformation

- Establish clear UK leadership in focus sectors (e.g. fintech, health AI).
- Demonstrate ethical AI as a proven competitive advantage.
- Ensure geographic distribution of benefits and opportunities.

Figure 8. Making it real: one possible implementation journey.

efforts in chapter 2 shows that early governance structures tend to persist and shape all subsequent development. Getting these right is more important than moving fast.

Governance

Establish an AI Coordination Authority, initially as a Cabinet Office unit reporting to the Prime Minister's Office, with a statutory mandate sought within eighteen months. First task: publish an AI Readiness Assessment across all major departments, modelled on the National Audit Office's digital maturity assessments but focused specifically on AI capability, data quality and workforce preparedness. Key design choice: whether this body coordinates (convenes, recommends, publishes) or directs (mandates, enforces, allocates). The UK's experience of coordination without enforcement, diagnosed in chapter 3, argues for meaningful directive powers from the outset.

Procurement

Issue updated procurement guidance mandating use of the Procurement Act 2023's competitive flexible procedure for all AI contracts above £500,000. Launch two outcome-based contracting pilots (for example, DWP benefit processing AI and HMRC compliance analytics) with built-in review stages and exit-by-design provisions.

Infrastructure

Finalize the location and technical specification for the Edinburgh exascale supercomputer. Begin procurement for an expansion of the UK's AIRR capacity. Publish the first annual Sovereign Compute Tracker showing what percentage of government AI workloads run on audit-capable infrastructure. Strategic choice: whether to pursue fully public sovereign compute or partnership models leveraging private investment. The sovereign compute analysis in chapter 4 frames this trade-off.

Skills

Extend the 'One Big Thing' AI training beyond foundational literacy to intermediate level for 50,000 civil servants in high-priority areas (DWP, HMRC, NHS, Home Office). Ring-fence 5% of AI Growth Zone infrastructure budgets for local skills development, connecting compute investment to regional capability building from the start.

International positioning

Prioritize establishing the UK's AI assurance and safety-testing credentials through the AI Security Institute. Begin developing responsible AI certification frameworks, choosing between comprehensive standards for global leadership and lighter-touch guidelines that evolve through experience. Deepen bilateral research partnerships, particularly where Brexit has created friction.

Phase two: scaling and testing (2027–8)

The second phase shifts from foundations to building infrastructure and capabilities at scale. This is where the tension between depth and breadth becomes acute: resources are finite, and every investment in one area is an investment not made elsewhere.

Governance
Seek primary legislation for the AI Coordination Authority if the Cabinet Office unit has demonstrated value. Published readiness assessments become annual, with departments required to respond publicly to findings. Strategic choice: whether to extend regulatory coherence through a single cross-sector AI framework or continue with the current principles-based approach interpreted differently by each sectoral regulator.

Procurement
Scale procurement reforms from two pilots to ten departments. Publish an outcome-based contract evaluation, including honest assessment of what did not work – practising the transparency this book advocates.

Infrastructure
Increase AIRR capacity to 10x baseline. First AI Growth Zone fully operational with integrated skills, compute and innovation ecosystem. Publish independent evaluation. Strategic choice: whether to impose data localization requirements for sensitive public-sector AI workloads (health, justice, welfare, national security), accepting the cost and complexity this creates.

Skills
AI skills levy pilot: extend the Apprenticeship Levy to cover AI reskilling for existing employees in five sectors. Evaluate take-up and employer response. Strategic choice: whether to protect skills funding through hypothecated mechanisms or continue competing through annual budget rounds – the 'Reality check' in chapter 5 frames why this matters.

International positioning
Standards development: choose between pursuing domain leadership (AI assurance, healthcare AI) or broader influence across the full AI governance landscape. Capacity-building investment: focus on Commonwealth nations, specific regions or global multilateral engagement.

Decision point (mid-2028): political continuity test

This falls within the likely general election window. The analysis of political discontinuity described earlier applies directly here. If the strategy is to survive a change of government, by this point it must have demonstrated measurable value in at least three high-visibility public services; built cross-party support through the multistakeholder governance forum; embedded AI capability deeply enough in departmental structures that reversal would be costly and visible; and created public expectation of continuation through tangible service improvements. Reforms that exist primarily as strategy documents will not survive. Reforms that citizens experience will.

Phase three: systemic embedding (2029–30)

The final phase transitions from building capabilities to embedding the UK's distinctive AI approach as institutional norm rather than programme overlay. By this point, the question is no longer whether the UK has an AI strategy but whether that strategy has become how institutions operate.

Governance

AI Coordination Authority operating with statutory mandate. Annual readiness assessments driving departmental AI strategies. Governance forum publishing an annual 'UK AI Implementation Report' with honest assessment of progress, failures and course corrections.

Procurement

Agile AI procurement is the default across government, not the exception. Exit-by-design provisions in all major platform contracts. Outcome-based evaluation embedded in standard contracting practice.

Infrastructure

Increase AIRR to 20x baseline. Sovereign Compute Tracker shows at least 50% of sensitive government AI workloads running on audit-capable infrastructure. At least three AI Growth Zones functioning as integrated skills-compute-innovation ecosystems, with independent evaluation of regional employment impact published.

Skills

Civil service at or approaching the 10% DDaT target. The skills levy (if piloted successfully) extended UK-wide. Regional digital skills consortia operational in every AI Growth Zone. Independent evaluation of whether skills investment has narrowed or widened the geographic gap in AI capability.

International positioning

The UK demonstrably leading in at least two of its five distinctive contributions identified in chapter 7: AI assurance as export industry, AI in complex public systems, mandatory algorithmic transparency, data trust models or binding infrastructure sovereignty provisions. Global recognition as the destination for responsible AI development and deployment.

This road map is ambitious but grounded in the evidence assembled across the preceding chapters. Its value lies not in the precision of individual targets (which will require adaptation as circumstances change) but in the integration of five delivery strands that are too often pursued in isolation, and in the explicit acknowledgement that strategic choices and political sustainability are as important as technical milestones. The principles established earlier in this chapter of momentum over perfection, contained experimentation, pull over push and simplicity under pressure should guide execution at every stage.

A note on credibility

Readers with experience of government, public services or large organizations will recognize that some of these targets are more achievable than others, and that the gap between a recommendation in a book and a reform in practice is precisely where previous strategies have failed. This book has tried to be honest about that gap throughout. Where a proposal builds on existing authority and infrastructure by mandating competitive flexible procurement under the 2023 Act, publishing AI readiness assessments, requiring exit-by-design provisions and so on, implementation is a matter of institutional willingness, not new legislation. Where a proposal requires primary legislation, sustained funding across spending review cycles or cultural change in how institutions relate to the communities they serve, the book says so and sequences it accordingly. The preceding road map is designed so that the achievable reforms come first and create the conditions (via the evidence, the capability, the political constituency) for the harder reforms that follow. Readers should judge it not by whether every target is met on schedule, but by whether the sequence is credible and the direction of travel is right.

What leaders must do differently

The road map sets out what needs to happen. But three areas require leadership choices that no road map can make. They involve choices where government, business, civil society and research institutions face trade-offs that are particularly difficult and cannot be resolved by better planning. Each demands that leaders accept short-term friction for long-term positioning.

For business leaders, AI adoption decisions that appear purely technical often carry strategic consequences that only become visible later. The depth of integration with particular platforms, the terms under which data is shared and the degree of dependency created all shape organizational options over time. Before deepening platform commitments, leaders should ask three questions: to what extent can we switch providers if circumstances change? Do we retain access to the data our systems generate? Can we meaningfully audit algorithmic decisions affecting our operations? Organizations that cannot answer these questions are making strategic choices by default and undoubtedly ceding future flexibility for present convenience.

For civil society, the test is whether participation in AI governance means real power or consultative theatre. Processes that seek input without conferring decision-making authority risk creating the appearance of inclusion without meaningful influence. For communities significantly affected by AI deployments in areas such as benefits administration, criminal justice and healthcare, consultative voice is insufficient. What is required is decision-making authority over deployments affecting vulnerable populations, resources to develop the technical expertise needed for informed engagement, and access to algorithmic audit results and impact assessments for independent oversight.

For research institutions, the challenge is translating globally competitive AI research into policy influence where it matters. As criticisms of the Alan Turing Institute's focus confirm,[6] excellence in publication does not automatically translate into impact on the UK's most pressing implementation challenges. Strengthening this connection requires embedded arrangements where researchers work within government departments on operational problems, research programmes focused explicitly on implementation barriers (organizational, political and cultural) alongside technical capability, and investment in the ability to communicate findings to policy audiences without sacrificing nuance.

A common thread connects these challenges. Meaningful progress in each case requires accepting friction: with powerful platform providers, with governance structures that resist sharing power and with academic incentive systems that reward publication over application. Democratic institutions tend to reward leaders who minimize conflict and avoid visible failures. Yet significant transformation rarely occurs without both. The question facing UK leadership is whether there is sufficient collective willingness to accept such discomfort, or whether AI strategy will join the accumulated pile of eloquent documents describing a future that never quite arrives.

Conclusions: implementation is the strategy

What gets implemented, in what sequence, with what resources, under whose accountability, these decisions constitute the real strategy regardless of what policy documents declare. When a government announces ambitious AI transformation plans but staffs the implementation team with junior analysts on temporary contracts, that communicates priorities more clearly than any white paper. When procurement rules remain unchanged despite commitments to agile delivery, that reveals which commitments are real. The preceding chapters have set out what the UK needs: reformed governance, sovereign infrastructure, new skills pipelines, ethical frameworks with institutional support, a distinctive international position and a phased road map to deliver them. Whether or not leaders treat implementation as the strategy itself rather than as a byproduct of having one will determine whether any of this occurs.

The UK has demonstrated it can deliver transformative change when urgency, capability and political will align. The Covid-19 vaccine rollout proved bureaucracy can move at speed. GDS showed that user needs can triumph over stakeholder preferences when principles are protected. Open Banking demonstrated that entrenched industries can be transformed through standards and determination. These were not accidents. They were the result of leaders choosing delivery over process, accepting imperfection in pursuit of progress and building capability to adapt rather than waiting for certainty.

The AI transformation ahead demands the same discipline. The tools exist, both technological and organizational. The knowledge exists, hard-won through decades of success and failure. The road map is set out in the preceding pages and a summary of the complete set of recommendations is consolidated in chapter 9. What remains is the willingness to start before conditions are perfect, to persist when progress seems slow and to hold leadership accountable for delivery rather than announcement. The work begins not with another strategy document but with the first difficult decision implemented on Monday morning.

CHAPTER 9

Summary of recommendations

This chapter draws together the book's principal recommendations into a single reference framework. The proposals are distributed across chapters 4 through 8, each embedded within the analytical argument that supports it. This summary is intended for readers who have absorbed that argument and want a consolidated view of what the book proposes, in a form suitable for briefings, planning and accountability.

The recommendations are organized under six headings: strategic positioning, governance reform, procurement, infrastructure, skills and workforce, ethics and legitimacy, and international positioning. These are followed by the phased implementation road map that sequences them across five years. Cross-references to the relevant chapters are provided throughout.

The chapter is designed to be read in two ways: as a continuous summary for those encountering the recommendations for the first time, and as a reference framework for those returning to specific proposals after reading the full argument. Readers preparing briefings or business cases should find the section headings and cross-references sufficient to locate the supporting evidence in the main text.

A note on credibility. Some of these proposals build on existing legislative authority and institutional infrastructure (mandating competitive flexible procurement under the 2023 Act, publishing AI readiness assessments and requiring exit-by-design provisions), where implementation is a matter of institutional willingness, not new legislation. Others require primary legislation, sustained funding across spending review cycles or cultural change in how institutions relate to the communities they serve. The book distinguishes between the two, and the road map is designed so that the achievable reforms come first and create the conditions (the evidence, the capability and the political constituency) for the harder reforms that follow.

Strategic positioning: the UK's adaptive path (chapters 1 and 7)

The book argues that the UK faces a choice between three fundamentally different approaches to AI, and that only the third plays to the UK's unique strengths.

- *The US innovation-first model.* This approach prioritizes speed, accepts platform dependency and relies on market forces. It produces extraordinary innovation but with extreme geographic concentration and risks low public trust.

- *The EU rights-first model.* This approach prioritizes citizen protection through comprehensive regulation, accepting slower adoption and higher compliance costs.

- *The UK's adaptive path (recommended).* This approach would build sovereign capability in areas that matter most, set governance standards that others adopt and use the UK's distinctive institutional assets as proving grounds for AI that is both innovative and accountable.

This is not a compromise position. It requires five specific commitments detailed below under international positioning, each involving political cost.

Governance reform (chapters 3 and 4)

Establish a statutory AI Coordination Authority modelled on the Office for Budget Responsibility: independent of departmental interests, with a statutory mandate, required to publish regular assessments and empowered to direct rather than merely coordinate. Initially a Cabinet Office unit reporting to the Prime Minister's Office, seeking statutory mandate within eighteen months. First task: publish an AI Readiness Assessment across all major departments. The critical design choice is between a body that coordinates (convenes, recommends and publishes) and one that directs (mandates, enforces and allocates). This book argues, on the basis of the evidence in chapter 3, that coordination without enforcement produces strategies that organizations politely endorse in principle and quietly ignore in practice (p. 93).

Redesign institutions around three principles. Adaptive capacity: distributed decision-making, embedded feedback loops, iterative learning with tolerance for failure and investment in durable human capability. Deep trust: transparency in design, clear accountability with real mechanisms for redress and responsiveness to evidence of harm. Authentic inclusion: from the start not as retrofit, with power not just voice, adequately resourced and measured with course correction (p. 72).

Adopt three governance models. Adaptive learning institutions built around cross-functional teams and failure documentation. Multistakeholder governance forums with mandated participation, modelled on the Open Banking precedent. Community-embedded innovation labs rooted in specific places and connected to a national network (p. 86).

Enable talent mobility across government, private sector, academia and civil society. Government must be able to recruit top talent without requiring permanent career commitment, and people must be able to move between sectors without sacrificing pension or seniority (p. 94).

Procurement reform (chapters 4 and 8)

Mandate the Procurement Act 2023's competitive flexible procedure for all AI contracts above £500,000, with built-in review stages (p. 91; p. 188).

Maximum two-year initial terms for all AI platform contracts with mandatory review before extension. Exit-by-design provisions in every major platform contract: data portability, architecture documentation and transition support that make switching providers feasible rather than theoretically possible (p. 91).

Outcome-based contracting pilots at DWP (benefit processing AI) and HMRC (compliance analytics) as initial candidates, evaluated on whether AI delivers intended outcomes rather than whether systems were deployed on schedule (p. 188).

Sovereign infrastructure (chapters 4 and 8)

Four design requirements drawn from international evidence: interoperability first (no critical information in isolated silos); privacy and security by design (radical transparency on data access, following the Estonian model); efficiency before scale (demonstrate value before imposing burdens); and inclusion as non-negotiable (robust offline alternatives, human support, clear audit trails) (p. 77).

Sovereignty by default as the direction of travel for the £250 billion in cross-Atlantic AI infrastructure investment, negotiated contract-by-contract and prioritizing the most sensitive functions. In practice, this means every major AI infrastructure agreement should include, at a minimum, a data residency clause for specified categories of sensitive data, a documented exit pathway with defined migration timescales and costs and audit access provisions that give UK regulators meaningful visibility into how systems operate. These are commercially standard provisions in other regulated sectors; the challenge is institutional willingness to insist on them. Data localization for the most sensitive public functions (health, justice, welfare and national security), where UK law must apply and UK regulators must be able to intervene without foreign consent. Multivendor, exit-friendly architectures using open standards (p. 80; p. 172).

Measurable target: at least 50% of sensitive government AI workloads running on audit-capable infrastructure by 2030, tracked through an annual Sovereign Compute Tracker (p. 191).

Skills and workforce (chapter 5)

A national Digital Lifelong Learning Passport. The UK has attempted portable skills records before – Individual Learning Accounts (collapsed amid fraud in 2001), the National Retraining Scheme (quietly abandoned) and the Lifelong Learning Entitlement (focused on funding access rather than skills portability). Each failed for different reasons, but none solved the demand-side problem: without employer recognition and individual incentive, no skills record is worth maintaining. The Passport proposed here is designed around those failures: employer co-investment giving firms a stake in the record's accuracy; government credits making maintenance financially worthwhile for individuals; and integration with existing platforms (particularly the Lifelong Learning Entitlement infrastructure) rather than building from scratch. It would track formal and informal achievements, linked to peer mentorship and project-based assessment (p. 112).

Cross-sector delivery alliances: regional digital skills consortia co-governed by employer coalitions, further education colleges, universities and civic partners; national digital skills observatories linking real-time labour market data with provider outcomes; microcredential and portfolio frameworks recognized across sectors (p. 113).

Digital citizenship from primary school covering not just technical skills but privacy, security, democracy and online identity (p. 114).

An AI skills levy extending the Apprenticeship Levy to cover AI reskilling for existing employees, with hypothecated digital skills funding ring-fenced from annual budget competition. Civil service target: an aspirational 10% of the workforce in digital, data and technology roles by 2030. (Whether the precise figure is 10%, 8% or 7% matters less than committing to a measurable trajectory and the workforce plan to achieve it.) In practice, the majority of growth will need to come from reclassifying and reskilling existing civil servants rather than net new recruitment. Near-term target: 50,000 civil servants trained to intermediate AI level in high-priority departments by the end of 2026, building on the 'One Big Thing' programme's foundational training (p. 117; p. 188).

Ethics and legitimacy (chapter 6)

Mandatory legitimacy assessment for every high-stakes public AI deployment: not only 'does this system produce accurate outputs?' but 'will the people affected by this system experience it as legitimate?'. There are several specific requirements.

Named human accountability for every consequential algorithmic decision via a specific individual, not a committee. A workable threshold must distinguish between decisions where AI determines or substantially shapes an outcome affecting an individual's rights, liberty, livelihood or access to essential services (where named accountability should apply) and decisions where AI assists human judgement without determining the outcome (where institutional accountability is sufficient). Defining this threshold should be an early task of the AI Coordination Authority, informed by consultation with deploying departments. The threshold will need revision as AI capabilities evolve, but an imperfect threshold is better than no threshold at all (p. 140).

Meaningful explanation rights in plain language delivered in time to matter rather than technical model documentation that only specialists can interrogate (p. 141).

Appropriate redress with clear consequences, independent of the deploying institution, resourced to investigate complaints seriously and empowered to compel changes to systems including suspension. The most credible institutional home is an expanded ICO, which already has jurisdiction over automated decision-making under UK GDPR. Extending the ICO's mandate to cover algorithmic redress for public-sector AI would build on existing capability rather than creating a new body, though it would require additional resources and possibly new statutory powers. An alternative is a specialist algorithmic ombudsman within the Parliamentary and Health Service Ombudsman's office. Either route is viable; leaving redress as an abstract requirement without specifying who delivers it is not (p. 141).

Give communities real power through workable mechanisms. Mandatory community impact assessments for all AI systems with significant public impact, sequenced before procurement decisions are made. The procuring authority must publish the assessment and respond formally to community concerns before awarding a contract and giving reasons where it proceeds despite objections. The model is environmental impact assessment, which has embedded community voice in planning decisions without giving any single group an absolute veto. Funded citizen panels with the power to require modification of AI deployments in specific localities, operating within defined timescales where a panel identifies evidence of disproportionate harm, the deploying institution must either modify the system or publish a detailed justification for proceeding. Affected-party representation with meaningful influence on the bodies that define requirements and evaluate proposals for high-impact public AI systems. Mandatory public registries of all algorithmic systems used in public-sector decision-making, with impact assessments and performance data (p. 142).

Invest in institutional ethics capacity. Trained ethics officers embedded in deploying organizations with authority to delay procurement. Regular adversarial testing of AI systems by independent bodies. Cross-sector learning networks sharing failure cases without reprisal (p. 143).

International positioning: five distinctive choices (chapter 7)

These are the commitments that give the UK's adaptive path concrete meaning. Each involves political cost; each prevents the 'third way' from becoming 'no way' (p. 169).

1. *AI assurance as an export industry.* The UK's research base, principles-based regulatory tradition and the AI Security Institute create a unique foundation for global leadership in AI testing, auditing and certification.

2. *AI in complex, high-trust public systems.* The NHS as a proving ground for AI that improves outcomes, maintains equity and commands public trust, creating a replicable model for dozens of countries.

3. *Mandatory algorithmic transparency for public-sector AI.* Publication of algorithmic impact assessments for all public-sector AI deployments, building on existing equalities legislation.

4. *Data trusts for sensitive public data.* Independent trusts with fiduciary obligations to data subjects, authorized to negotiate terms with AI developers.

5. *Binding infrastructure sovereignty provisions.* 'Sovereignty by default' as the direction of travel for incoming cross-Atlantic AI investment, negotiated into specific contracts with priority given to the most sensitive public functions.

Target: the UK demonstrably leading in at least two of these five areas by 2030 (p. 191).

Implementation road map (chapter 8)

The road map sequences these recommendations across five delivery strands (governance, procurement, infrastructure, skills, international positioning) in three phases. It is offered as one credible path rather than the only possible one; its value lies in the integration of strands too often pursued in isolation and in the explicit identification of decision points where leaders will face critical trade-offs.

Phase 1: foundations (2026–7)

Establish the AI Coordination Authority as a Cabinet Office unit reporting to the Prime Minister's Office. Publish an AI Readiness Assessment across all major departments, modelled on the National Audit Office's digital maturity assessments but focused specifically on AI implementation capability. Issue updated procurement guidance mandating competitive flexible procedure for all AI contracts above £500,000. Launch two outcome-based contracting pilots at DWP and HMRC with built-in review stages. Finalize Edinburgh exascale supercomputer specification and begin expanded AIRR procurement. Publish first annual Sovereign Compute Tracker. Extend civil service AI training to intermediate level for 50,000 staff in high-priority areas (DWP, HMRC, NHS, Home Office). Ring-fence 5% of AI Growth Zone infrastructure budgets for local skills development. Begin building AI assurance credentials through the AI Safety Institute and develop responsible AI certification frameworks.

Phase 2: scaling and testing (2027–8)

Seek primary legislation for the AI Coordination Authority. Scale procurement reforms to ten departments. First AI Growth Zone fully operational. Pilot the AI skills levy in five sectors. Key decision points: whether to impose data localization requirements for sensitive public-sector AI workloads; whether to protect skills funding through hypothecated mechanisms. A critical political continuity test falls in mid-2028, within the likely general election window. By that point the strategy must have demonstrated measurable value in at least three high-visibility public services, built constituencies extending beyond the originating government and created institutional structures whose removal would be politically costly.

Phase 3: systemic embedding (2029–30)

AI Coordination Authority operating with statutory mandate. Annual 'UK AI Implementation Report' published with honest assessment of progress, failures and course corrections. Agile AI procurement the default across government, not the exception. Exit-by-design provisions in all major platform contracts. Outcome-based evaluation embedded in standard contracting practice. AIRR capacity at 20x baseline. Sovereign Compute Tracker showing at least 50% of sensitive government AI workloads on audit-capable infrastructure. At least three AI Growth Zones functioning as integrated skills-compute-innovation ecosystems with independent evaluation of regional employment and capability impact. Civil service at or approaching the DDaT target. Skills levy extended UK-wide. Regional digital skills consortia operational in every AI Growth Zone. UK demonstrably leading in at least two of its five distinctive global contributions, with global recognition as the preferred partner for responsible AI deployment.

A final note

Readers with experience of government, public services or large organizations will recognize that some of these proposals are more achievable than others. Where a recommendation builds on existing legislative authority and institutional infrastructure (mandating competitive flexible procurement, publishing readiness assessments and requiring exit-by-design provisions), implementation is a matter of institutional willingness, not new legislation. Where a recommendation requires primary legislation, sustained cross-cycle funding or cultural change in how institutions relate to the communities they serve, the book says so and sequences it accordingly. The road map is designed so that the achievable reforms come first and create the conditions for the harder reforms that follow.

These recommendations are deliberately more demanding than conventional AI policy prescriptions. They must be, because two decades of evidence, assembled across the preceding chapters, demonstrate that conventional prescriptions have not worked. At the same time, this book recognizes that public service reform operates under constraints that the private sector does not face: democratic accountability, universal service obligations, legacy infrastructure, electoral cycles and political incentive structures that actively punish the adaptive behaviour successful transformation demands. Every recommendation in this chapter must be read against that reality. The question is not whether reform is difficult (it self-evidently is), but whether the alternative of continued strategic ambition without institutional change is acceptable.

The UK does not need to build its own foundation models to exercise sovereignty over AI. It needs to be a disciplined, coordinated buyer that consolidates demand with the same institutional authority that GDS once wielded for digital, while insisting on the multivendor architectures, interoperability standards and exit provisions that keep genuine optionality alive. That is the UK's distinctive path: neither the US model of market dominance, the EU model of regulatory primacy, nor the Chinese model of state direction, but the smart-buyer model that the UK has already proved it can execute. The question is whether it will choose to do so again, at higher stakes and in a more complex geopolitical environment.

APPENDIX

International AI strategies

This appendix provides the evidence base supporting chapter 7's analysis of international AI strategies. The dominant models (US innovation-first, EU rights-first and China's state-directed approach) are summarized with key data points; chapter 7 provides the full analytical treatment. The small-nation profiles that follow offer more detailed case studies of focused strategies that demonstrate what the UK might learn from countries that have achieved outsized impact through deliberate prioritization.

The three dominant models: key data

United States: the innovation-first model

The US approach prioritizes rapid innovation through minimal regulation and market-led development, trusting that ethics and equity can be addressed after technological breakthroughs rather than constraining innovation upfront. The model relies on sectoral regulation (e.g. the Food and Drug Administration for medical AI and the Securities and Exchange Commission for financial algorithms) rather than comprehensive frameworks. Public investment is substantial: \$2.6 billion across twenty-five National AI Research Institutes and \$280 billion through the CHIPS Act. But private sector funding dominates, exceeding

$150 billion in 2024 alone. The Defense Advanced Research Projects Agency's high-risk, high-reward research model and Silicon Valley's venture ecosystem enable rapid scaling from concept to global platform.

Results

US companies dominate global AI platforms and hold an estimated 22% of global AI patents. However, the model produces significant costs alongside its innovation: algorithmic bias in criminal justice systems, healthcare AI disparities affecting minority communities and extreme geographic concentration with 75% of investment in just three states. Most critically, only 37% of Americans trust technology companies, with AI creating a legitimacy deficit that may constrain long-term adoption.

European Union: the rights-first model

The EU has taken the opposite approach, constructing comprehensive regulatory frameworks before significant deployment. The AI Act, coming into force in 2024–6, creates a risk-based pyramid – from prohibited uses through to high-risk applications – requiring strict compliance to minimal-risk systems with no additional requirements. Conformity assessments, CE marking and national supervisory authorities coordinated by a European AI Board enforce the framework, with fines reaching 6% of global turnover. Implementation varies significantly across member states: France emphasizes sovereign AI with a €1.5 billion investment, Germany focuses on industrial applications with €5 billion invested through 2025, while the Netherlands mandates algorithmic impact assessments.

Results

The EU achieves high public trust, with 68% of citizens supporting AI regulation, creating market certainty for ethical AI companies. However, between 2020 and 2024 the EU's share of global

AI patents declined from 12% to 8%, compliance costs averaged €500,000 for high-risk certification and 18% of EU AI researchers relocated. The framework provides protection but may be constraining the innovation it seeks to govern.

China: the state-directed model

China's approach demonstrates what concentrated state resources can achieve, targeting global AI leadership by 2030 through coordinated investment and deployment across all economic sectors. The 2017 New Generation AI Development Plan coordinates national champions such as Baidu, Alibaba and Tencent alongside city-level AI zones and military–civil fusion for dual-use technologies. The social credit system represents large-scale AI deployment affecting daily life for 1.4 billion people. State coordination enables rapid scaling and experimentation that would be impossible in democratic contexts.

Results

China leads with an estimated 38% of global AI patents and dominates facial recognition with eight of the top ten companies globally. Manufacturing AI achieves 35% productivity gains in pilot factories. However, 540 million surveillance cameras and the social credit system raise severe human rights concerns that are incompatible with democratic values. China's drive to create its own complete AI technology stack (chips, software frameworks and models), accelerated by US export controls, demonstrates both the power of strategic coordination and the risks of decoupling.

Focused excellence: small-nation strategies

Beyond the three dominant models, smaller nations demonstrate that focused strategies can achieve global impact without matching larger nations' resources. Four cases offer lessons for any country seeking to punch above its weight.

Estonia: comprehensive digital transformation

With 1.3 million people, Estonia has achieved what the UK struggles with at 67 million. X-Road, the national data exchange layer, enables 99% of public services to be online. Every citizen has a mandatory digital ID. The 'once-only' principle means that citizens provide information once and government reuses it across services. Radical transparency ensures that citizens see every government use of their data, including the official's name. This was not achieved overnight, taking Estonia more than thirty years to build, from basic registries through infrastructure to proactive services that anticipate citizen needs.

Results

It is claimed that 2% of GDP is saved annually through digital efficiency. Companies can be established online in eight minutes. 99% of prescriptions are processed digitally and there have been zero reported cases of identity theft through digital ID. Three elements underpin this: technical interoperability enforced ruthlessly, radical transparency creating trust and long-term consistency across political cycles.

Singapore: strategic focus through 'peaks'

Singapore's National AI Strategy 2.0 demonstrates global leadership through radical prioritization. Rather than competing everywhere, Singapore identified specific 'peaks of excellence' in urban solutions, trade and logistics, and finance where it could achieve global dominance. Fifteen concrete actions include attracting 500 top 'AI creators' globally, scaling AI practitioners from 5,000 to 15,000 and establishing Southeast Asia's AI hub. S$1 billion direct investment leverages S$3 billion in private coinvestment.

Results

Up to 20% AI adoption rates. 74% public trust through visible benefit sharing and extensive consultation. The '100 Startups Program' provides patient capital and guaranteed government contracts, derisking innovation.

Denmark: participatory governance

Denmark's approach emphasizes consensus-building through formal social partnership structures. Government–union digital transformation agreements ensure workforce support. Citizen panels have binding influence on AI deployment. The TechPact sees industry commit to creating 10,000 tech jobs while government provides reskilling for 50,000 workers. AI literacy is integrated into primary education. Lifelong Learning Accounts provide DKK 10,000 annually per citizen for skills development.

Results

92% digital service usage. 87% citizen satisfaction. 12% public-sector productivity gains. 4.2% unemployment despite automation.

Canada: operationalizing ethics

Canada pioneered making AI ethics operational through mandatory algorithmic impact assessments for all government AI. Risk scoring based on impact severity determines the requirements: high-risk systems require peer review and public disclosure; mandatory human-in-the-loop for critical decisions ensures accountability. Canada also uniquely recognizes Indigenous data sovereignty through OCAP principles (ownership, control, access and possession).

Results

Sixty-seven systems assessed in two years. 23% required modification. 8% rejected as too high-risk. 94% civil servant compliance.

Conclusions

The international landscape offers no perfect model for the UK to copy, but rather a rich set of experiences to learn from. The US demonstrates innovation dynamism but social costs. The EU provides citizen protection but innovation constraints. China shows state coordination's power but democratic incompatibility. Smaller nations prove that focused excellence beats resource scale.

The UK's opportunity lies not in choosing between these models but in synthesizing their strengths while avoiding their weaknesses. With the right choices, the UK can demonstrate that democratic values, innovation excellence and social inclusion are not trade-offs but mutually reinforcing elements of sustainable AI transformation.

Key sources

United States

Defense Advanced Research Projects Agency. 2018. AI next campaign: multi-year investment in artificial intelligence research and development. Programme Announcement (https://www.darpa.mil/research/programs/ai-next-campaign).

Defense Advanced Research Projects Agency. 2023. AI forward initiative: new directions for artificial intelligence research. Programme Description (https://www.darpa.mil/research/programs/ai-forward).

National Science Foundation. 2022. CHIPS and Science overview: historic investments in research and innovation. Implementation Guidance (https://www.nsf.gov/chips).

National Science Foundation. 2023. NSF announces 7 new National Artificial Intelligence Research Institutes. Press Release, 4 May (https://www.nsf.gov/news/nsf-announces-7-new-national-artificial).

National Science Foundation. 2025. FY2025 annual report on the status of the AI Institutes. Report to Congress (https://www.nitrd.gov/pubs/FY25-National-AI-Institutes.pdf).

US Congress. 2022. HR 4346: CHIPS and Science Act of 2022. Public Law 117-167 (https://www.govtrack.us/congress/bills/117/hr4346).

White House. 2022. FACT SHEET: CHIPS and Science Act will lower costs, create jobs, strengthen supply chains, and counter China. Policy Summary (https://bidenwhitehouse.archives.gov/briefing-room/statements-releases/2022/08/09/fact-sheet-chips-and-science-act-will-lower-costs-create-jobs-strengthen-supply-chains-and-counter-china/).

European Union

European Commission. 2025. European approach to artificial intelligence. Policy Overview (https://digital-strategy.ec.europa.eu/en/policies/european-approach-artificial-intelligence).

European Parliament and Council. 2024. Regulation (EU) 2024/1689: laying down harmonised rules on artificial intelligence (Artificial Intelligence Act). Legislation (https://eur-lex.europa.eu/eli/reg/2024/1689/oj/eng).

Gallo, Valeria, and Suchitra Nair. 2024. EU AI Act: forging a strategic response. Article, 13 September, Deloitte (https://www.deloitte.com/uk/en/blogs/ecrs/eu-ai-act-forging-a-strategic-response.html).

China

Arcesati, Rebecca. 2023. China's AI development model in an era of technological deglobalization. Research Report, May, Merics (https://merics.org/en/report/chinas-ai-development-model-era-technological-deglobalization).

European Parliament. 2021. China's ambitions in artificial intelligence. Research Briefing (https://www.europarl.europa.eu/

RegData/etudes/ATAG/2021/696206/EPRS_ATA(2021)696206_EN.pdf).

Sheehan, Matt. 2023. China's AI regulations and how they get made. Working Paper, July, Carnegie Endowment for International Peace (https://carnegieendowment.org/research/2023/07/chinas-ai-regulations-and-how-they-get-made).

Estonia

e-Estonia. nd. X-Road: interoperability services. Government Information Page (https://e-estonia.com/solutions/interoperability-services/x-road/).

GovTech Intelligence Hub. 2025. Smarter data exchange: how X-Road became a model for digital public infrastructure. Case Study, 18 June (https://www.govtechintelhub.org/case-study-details/smarter-data-exchange:-how-x-road-became-a-model-for-digital-public-infrastructure/aJYTG0000000014AA).

Hardy, Alex. 2024. Estonia's digital diplomacy: Nordic interoperability and the challenges of cross-border e-governance. *Internet Policy Review* 13(3) (https://policyreview.info/articles/analysis/estonias-digital-diplomacy-nordic-interoperability).

Singapore

Government of the Republic of Singapore. 2023. National Artificial Intelligence Strategy 2.0: AI for the public good, for Singapore and the world. National Strategy, 4 December (https://file.go.gov.sg/nais2023.pdf).

Denmark

Danish Government. 2018. Strategy for Denmark's digital growth. National Strategy, February (https://investindk.com/insights/the-danish-government-presents-digital-growth-strategy).

Danish Government. 2022. National strategy for digitalisation. National Strategy, May (https://en.digst.dk/media/mndfou2j/national-strategy-for-digitalisation-together-in-the-digital-development.pdf).

Canada

Treasury Board of Canada Secretariat. 2019, as amended. Directive on automated decision-making. Government Directive (https://www.tbs-sct.canada.ca/pol/doc-eng.aspx?id=32592).

Treasury Board of Canada Secretariat. 2024. Algorithmic impact assessment tool. Assessment Tool (https://www.canada.ca/en/government/system/digital-government/digital-government-innovations/responsible-use-ai/algorithmic-impact-assessment.html).

Acknowledgements

Bringing together this book has required an immense amount of work. Especially as so much has happened recently in the world of AI and digital technology. Fortunately, I have been able to draw on an extensive body of work from the past few years. By building on previous writing, this book revises and rejuvenates many of the observations that I have made over more than two decades on the promises and pitfalls of digital transformation. Common themes are extracted and new ideas explored.

As a result, several of the key ideas presented in this book owe a significant debt to earlier work carried out with input from many colleagues, including Nawtej Dosanjh, Jerry Fishenden, Liz-Ann Gayle, James Herbert, Jon Holt, David Lopez, Roger Maull, Rashik Parmar, Tony Moretta, Travis Street, Mark Thompson, Dave West, Chad Bond and Zena Wood. I will always be indebted to these individuals for their knowledge and generosity and for the many things they have taught me.

A note on the use of AI tools

This book is the result of a great deal of work over many years. It draws on ideas, conversations, research and writings that have occupied a large part of my working life. To bring this together I have made extensive use of AI tools throughout the writing process. This included reviewing and summarizing works I have previously produced, identifying common themes and gaps, synthesizing multiple sources into a coherent thread, and reviewing materials for completeness, correctness and coherence. It also extended to drafting new text, analysing external sources against the manuscript's arguments, critically reviewing recommendations for credibility and implementability, and suggesting structural and editorial improvements. In short, AI tools served as a research assistant, drafting partner and critical reader throughout the book's development. To do this I employed a variety of AI tools and capabilities, including (but not limited to) ChatGPT, Claude, Gemini, Perplexity/Comet and Cursor.

Throughout my focus has been to ensure that these tools are used appropriately, judiciously and effectively. Every argument, recommendation and judgement in this book reflects my own analysis and experience; all AI-generated text has been personally reviewed, revised and in many cases substantially rewritten to ensure accuracy, consistency and alignment with the book's analytical framework. I accept full responsibility for this content.

About the author

Alan is a professor in digital economy, an experienced business executive and a strategic advisor. He has spent more than thirty years in the US, Europe and the UK driving large-scale software-driven programmes with commercial high-tech companies, leading R&D teams, building state-of-the-art solutions and improving software product delivery approaches.

Alan now engages in business consulting, advisory work and research with a variety of organizations across many sectors. Alan holds a professorship in digital economy at the University of Exeter, where he co-founded Exeter's initiative in the digital economy (INDEX). In addition, he leads AI activity for the Digital Leaders network (a community of more than 65,000 digital practitioners) and the Digital Policy Alliance (an advisory body supporting peers in the UK House of Lords). Alan is a fellow of the British Computer Society and recently completed a fellowship at the Alan Turing Institute, the UK's national institute for data science and AI.

Alan has written a wide variety of books and papers on topics such as enterprise software engineering, systems design, agile delivery and digital business transformation. Alan's latest work explores the growing impact of AI on business and how to deliver AI-at-Scale.

Further details about this book and its content can be found at FutureOfAI.uk. More information about Alan's work and publications can be found at www.AlanBrown.net.

Notes

All links valid as of 20 March 2026.

Chapter 1

1 https://time.com/7318214/trump-starmer-us-uk-tech-prosperity-deal-signed/
2 https://www.cnbc.com/2025/09/16/tech-giants-to-pour-billions-into-uk-ai-heres-what-we-know-so-far.html
3 https://aimagazine.com/news/google-opens-5bn-uk-data-centre-to-boost-ai-economy
4 https://www.cnbc.com/2025/09/16/tech-giants-to-pour-billions-into-uk-ai-heres-what-we-know-so-far.html
5 https://www.gov.uk/government/publications/ai-opportunities-action-plan/ai-opportunities-action-plan
6 https://www.gov.uk/government/news/north-east-england-set-for-billions-in-investment-and-thousands-of-jobs-as-uk-and-us-ink-tech-partnership
7 https://uk.finance.yahoo.com/news/uk-us-tech-deal-ai-trump-starmer-state-visit-033014872.html
8 https://www.itpro.com/business/policy-and-legislation/uks-tech-prosperity-deal-with-us-hits-rocky-ground
9 https://www.theguardian.com/technology/2025/jun/06/high-court-tells-uk-lawyers-to-urgently-stop-misuse-of-ai-in-legal-work
10 https://academic.oup.com/pnasnexus/article/4/10/pgaf316/8303888
11 https://hai.stanford.edu/ai-index
12 https://news.sky.com/story/uk-to-become-ai-maker-not-taker-says-sir-keir-starmer-13381107
13 https://www.nao.org.uk/insights/initial-learning-from-the-governments-response-to-the-covid-19-pandemic/
14 https://www.thelancet.com/journals/lancet/article/PIIS0140-6736(11)61275-0/fulltext

15 https://cacm.acm.org/news/how-software-bugs-led-to-one-of-the-greatest-miscarriages-of-justice-in-british-history/

16 https://bigbrotherwatch.org.uk/wp-content/uploads/2021/07/Poverty-Panopticon.pdf

17 https://www.local.gov.uk/publications/state-digital-local-government

18 https://pubmed.ncbi.nlm.nih.gov/28166675/

19 https://hbr.org/2025/01/how-to-marry-process-management-and-ai

20 https://www.economist.com/leaders/2017/05/06/the-worlds-most-valuable-resource-is-no-longer-oil-but-data

21 Harper, Richard H. R. 2025. *The Shape of Thought: Reasoning in the Age of AI*. McGill-Queen's University Press.

22 Larson, Erik J. 2021. *The Myth of Artificial Intelligence: Why Computers Can't Think the Way We Do*. Belknap Press.

23 March, James G. 1994. *A Primer on Decision Making: How Decisions Happen*. Free Press.

Chapter 2

1 https://www.gov.uk/government/publications/state-of-digital-government-review

2 https://ntouk.wordpress.com/wp-content/uploads/2015/06/government-direct.pdf

3 https://www.cl.cam.ac.uk/archive/rja14/Papers/npfit-mpp-2014-case-history.pdf

4 https://onlinelibrary.wiley.com/doi/abs/10.1111/j.1467-9299.1991.tb00797.x

5 https://www.nao.org.uk/reports/improving-it-procurement-the-impact-of-the-office-of-government-commerces-initiatives-on-departments-and-suppliers-in/

6 Ibid.

7 https://www.researchgate.net/publication/262253744_Beyond_the_IT_Productivity_Paradox

8 https://www.bbc.co.uk/programmes/w3ct7477

9 https://www.goldmansachs.com/intelligence/pages/gen-ai-too-much-spend-too-little-benefit.html

10 https://dl.acm.org/doi/10.1145/3630024

11 https://www.nao.org.uk/reports/digital-transformation-in-government/

12 https://post.parliament.uk/covid-19-and-the-digital-divide/

13 https://committees.parliament.uk/committee/430/public-services-committee/news/123559/lessons-from-covid19-major-report-on-public-services-launched/
14 https://www.nao.org.uk/reports/digital-transformation-in-government-addressing-the-barriers/
15 https://www.gov.uk/government/publications/state-of-digital-government-review
16 https://time.com/6102902/london-fintech/
17 Ibid.
18 https://www.openbanking.org.uk/what-is-open-banking/
19 https://link.springer.com/article/10.1057/s41261-024-00262-x
20 https://www.nao.org.uk/reports/the-use-of-digital-technology-in-the-nhs/
21 https://publications.parliament.uk/pa/cm5803/cmselect/cmhealth/223/report.html
22 https://lordslibrary.parliament.uk/creative-industries-growth-jobs-and-productivity/
23 https://assets.publishing.service.gov.uk/media/685943ddb328f1ba50f3cf15/industrial_strategy_creative_industries_sector_plan.pdf
24 https://www.makeuk.org/insights/reports/making-it-smarter-global-lessons-accelerating-automation-digital-adoption-uk
25 https://institute.global/insights/tech-and-digitalisation/from-startup-to-scaleup-turning-uk-innovation-into-prosperity-and-power
26 https://report.technation.io/
27 https://www.datacenterdynamics.com/en/news/report-finds-28-of-uks-central-govt-it-still-considered-legacy/
28 https://www.crowncommercial.gov.uk/agreements/RM1557.14
29 https://www.icaew.com/insights/viewpoints-on-the-news/2024/sep-2024/sme-public-sector-procurement-spend-stalls-despite-pledges
30 https://fortune.com/2025/08/18/mit-report-95-percent-generative-ai-pilots-at-companies-failing-cfo/
31 https://institute.global/insights/public-services/the-nhs-at-a-crossroads-the-app-that-can-transform-britains-health
32 https://www.nao.org.uk/reports/use-of-artificial-intelligence-in-government/
33 https://www.bcg.com/press/24october2024-ai-adoption-in-2024-74-of-companies-struggle-to-achieve-and-scale-value
34 https://www.theguardian.com/society/2018/jun/15/universal-credit-savaged-by-public-spending-watchdog-nao

Chapter 3

1 https://www.gov.uk/government/publications/national-ai-strategy
2 https://www.cio.com/article/3850763/88-of-ai-pilots-fail-to-reach-production-but-thats-not-all-on-it.html
3 https://www.gov.uk/government/publications/digital-id-scheme-explainer/digital-id-scheme-explainer
4 https://transform.england.nhs.uk/ai-lab/
5 https://www.gov.uk/government/news/millions-of-customers-benefit-as-open-banking-reaches-milestone
6 https://www.theguardian.com/technology/2017/jul/03/google-deepmind-16m-patient-royal-free-deal-data-protection-act
7 https://www.legislation.gov.uk/ukpga/2025/18/contents
8 https://www.lawsociety.org.uk/topics/news/the-law-society-welcomes-data-act-but-raises-concerns
9 https://www.theregister.com/2025/02/14/uk_ai_security_institute/

Chapter 4

1 https://assets.publishing.service.gov.uk/media/65c0b6bd63a23d0013c821a0/implementing_the_uk_ai_regulatory_principles_guidance_for_regulators.pdf
2 https://committees.parliament.uk/committee/127/public-accounts-committee/news/98272/government-flagship-digital-identification-system-failing-its-users/
3 https://institute.global/insights/public-services/the-nhs-at-a-crossroads-the-app-that-can-transform-britains-health
4 https://www.adalovelaceinstitute.org/blog/the-role-of-public-compute/
5 https://www.gov.uk/government/publications/ai-opportunities-action-plan/ai-opportunities-action-plan
6 https://www.gov.uk/government/publications/uk-compute-roadmap/uk-compute-roadmap
7 https://www.bain.com/insights/deepseek-a-game-changer-in-ai-efficiency/
8 https://www.fca.org.uk/firms/future-open-banking-joint-regulatory-oversight-committee
9 https://www.legislation.gov.uk/ukpga/2023/54/contents
10 https://www.gov.uk/digital-marketplace
11 https://www.turing.ac.uk/news/publications/ai-governance-around-world-uk

Chapter 5

1. https://www.nao.org.uk/reports/the-digital-skills-gap-in-government-survey-findings/
2. https://dl.acm.org/doi/10.1145/3630024
3. https://www.nao.org.uk/reports/the-national-programme-for-it-in-the-nhs-an-update-on-the-delivery-of-detailed-care-records-systems/
4. https://www.gov.uk/government/publications/independent-investigation-of-the-nhs-in-england
5. https://creativeindustriesclusters.com/creative-clusters-the-story-so-far-2021/
6. https://www.ons.gov.uk/peoplepopulationandcommunity/householdcharacteristics/homeinternetandsocialmediausage/articles/exploringtheuksdigitaldivide/2019-03-03
7. https://www.nesta.org.uk/blog/neglecting-digital-natives-risks-uks-economic-future/
8. https://www.harveynash.co.uk/latest-news/digital-leadership-report-2025
9. https://www.gov.uk/government/publications/digital-skills-for-the-uk-economy
10. https://computingqualityframework.org/
11. https://post.parliament.uk/research-briefings/post-pn-0725/
12. https://www.theguardian.com/world/2025/mar/09/the-pandemic-reinforced-existing-inequalities-it-was-a-magnifying-glass-how-covid-changed-britain
13. https://www.england.nhs.uk/blog/digital-nurse-network-supporting-nurses-across-the-nhs/
14. https://www.gov.uk/government/publications/fit-for-the-future-10-year-health-plan-for-england and https://nhsproviders.org/learning-from-digital-successes-and-failures
15. https://financialservicesskills.org/wp-content/uploads/2025/11/FSSC_Future_Skills_Report_2025.pdf
16. https://ukdataservice.ac.uk/case-study/creative-clusters-in-the-uk/
17. https://media.nesta.org.uk/documents/the_geography_of_creativity_in_the_uk.pdf
18. https://www.nao.org.uk/reports/digital-transformation-in-government-addressing-the-barriers/
19. https://www.civilserviceworld.com/professions/article/civil-servants-ai-training-one-big-thing-2025
20. https://governmentdigitalanddatahub.campaign.gov.uk/learn/get-tech-certified/

21 https://ddat-capability-framework.service.gov.uk/
22 https://www.local.gov.uk/our-support/cyber-digital-and-technology/12-local-government-digitalisation-outcomes
23 https://www.gravitasgroup.co.uk/tech-salary-survey-2025
24 https://www.techtalentcharter.co.uk/reports/diversity-in-tech-report-2024/
25 https://www.ons.gov.uk/peoplepopulationandcommunity/householdcharacteristics/homeinternetandsocialmediausage/articles/exploringtheuksdigitaldivide/2019-03-04
26 https://www.gov.uk/government/publications/blackpool-connectivity-and-tourism-a-lffn-case-study/blackpool-connectivity-and-tourism-case-study
27 https://pec.ac.uk/wp-content/uploads/2024/07/Beyond-growth-promoting-inclusive-development-of-creative-clusters-in-the-UK-Creative-PEC-Research-Report-July-2024.pdf
28 https://www.tandfonline.com/doi/full/10.1080/17510694.2023.221070
29 https://assets.publishing.service.gov.uk/media/5a7b1c2240f0b66a2fc053a3/171107_The_experiences_of_those_in_the_gig_economy.pdf
30 https://feweek.co.uk/bootcamps-fray-and-wear-thin-as-providers-begin-race-to-the-bottom/
31 https://www.forbes.com/sites/gradsoflife/2021/11/03/rethinking-the-so-called-skills-gap
32 https://www.nao.org.uk/reports/individual-learning-accounts/
33 https://feweek.co.uk/flagship-retraining-service-scrapped-after-pilot-flopped/
34 https://www.hepi.ac.uk/2025/10/28/what-does-the-post-16-education-and-skills-white-paper-say-about-access-and-participation/
35 https://digital-strategy.ec.europa.eu/en/factpages/estonia-2025-digital-decade-country-report
36 https://investindk.com/-/media/websites/invest-in-denmark/files/danish-digital-growth-strategy2018.ashx
37 https://www.skillsfuture.gov.sg/
38 https://cddo.blog.gov.uk/2025/03/13/techtrack-revolutionising-digital-apprenticeships-in-the-civil-service/

Chapter 6

1 https://medconfidential.org/whats-the-story/care-data-2013-2016/
2 https://www.disabilityrightsuk.org/news/2019/july/one-three-capita-pip-assessments-found-have-significant-flaws

3 https://assets.publishing.service.gov.uk/media/5a7c658ee5274a7ee256730f/6683.pdf
4 https://publications.parliament.uk/pa/ld201719/ldselect/ldai/100/10014.htm
5 https://www.gov.uk/government/publications/the-centre-for-data-ethics-and-innovations-approach-to-the-governance-of-data-driven-technology
6 https://gdpr-info.eu/
7 https://www.gov.uk/government/news/cdei-proposes-a-roadmap-to-tackle-algorithmic-bias
8 Weizenbaum, Joseph. 1976. *Computer Power and Human Reason: From Judgment to Calculation*. W.H. Freeman.
9 https://www.adalovelaceinstitute.org/report/algorithmic-accountability-public-sector/
10 https://digital.nhs.uk/services/nhs-pathways
11 https://www.gov.uk/government/news/ai-to-be-trialled-at-unprecedented-scale-across-nhs-screening
12 https://link.springer.com/article/10.1186/s12910-025-01243-z
13 https://www.bbc.co.uk/news/health-26259101
14 https://link.springer.com/article/10.1186/s12910-025-01243-z
15 https://www.bis.org/publ/mktc09.htm
16 https://pmc.ncbi.nlm.nih.gov/articles/PMC8978471/
17 https://www.lendingstandardsboard.org.uk/uk-ethnic-minority-led-businesses-far-less-likely-to-have-full-loan-applications-approved-than-other-businesses-lsb-research/
18 https://www.fca.org.uk/news/news-stories/launch-permanent-digital-sandbox
19 https://financialservicesskills.org/
20 https://www.libertyhumanrights.org.uk/issue/policing-by-machine/
21 https://www.amnesty.org.uk/press-releases/uk-police-forces-supercharging-racism-crime-predicting-tech-new-report
22 https://www.techuk.org/resource/all-you-need-to-know-about-ai-adoption-in-criminal-justice.html
23 https://www.transformjustice.org.uk/news-insight/computer-says-no-bail-does-ai-reduce-or-increase-human-bias/
24 https://theodi.org/news-and-events/blog/what-can-we-learn-from-the-qualifications-fiasco/
25 https://www.gov.uk/government/calls-for-evidence/generative-artificial-intelligence-in-education-call-for-evidence

26 https://www.gov.uk/government/publications/curriculum-and-assessment-review-final-report
27 https://www.legislation.gov.uk/ukpga/2018/12/contents
28 https://gdpr-info.eu/
29 https://www.gov.uk/government/publications/ai-regulation-a-pro-innovation-approach/white-paper

Chapter 7

1 https://www.pewresearch.org/internet/2025/04/03/how-the-us-public-and-ai-experts-view-artificial-intelligence/
2 https://www.bbc.co.uk/news/articles/crmddnge9yro
3 https://www.gibsondunn.com/two-weeks-in-key-trump-administration-developments-in-tech-policy/
4 https://www.skadden.com/insights/publications/2025/12/white-house-launches-national-framework
5 https://www.gov.uk/government/news/memorandum-of-understanding-between-the-government-of-the-united-states-of-america-and-the-government-of-the-united-kingdom-of-great-britain-and-north
6 https://www.itpro.com/business/policy-and-legislation/uks-tech-prosperity-deal-with-us-hits-rocky-ground
7 https://www.brookings.edu/articles/controlling-cambridge-analytica-managing-the-new-risks-of-personal-data-collection/
8 https://ec.europa.eu/eurostat/web/products-eurostat-news/w/ddn-20250123-3
9 https://datainnovation.org/2021/07/how-much-will-the-artificial-intelligence-act-cost-europe/
10 https://www.ipinst.org/2016/05/information-technology-and-governance-estonia
11 https://digichina.stanford.edu/work/full-translation-chinas-new-generation-artificial-intelligence-development-plan-2017/
12 https://www.bruegel.org/policy-brief/how-deepseek-has-changed-artificial-intelligence-and-what-it-means-europe
13 https://www.gov.uk/government/publications/ai-opportunities-action-plan
14 https://institute.global/insights/tech-and-digitalisation/a-new-national-purpose-accelerating-uk-science-in-the-age-of-ai
15 https://www.gov.uk/government/publications/uk-science-and-technology-framework
16 https://www.foreignaffairs.com/united-states/ai-divide

17 Ibid.
18 https://www.turing.ac.uk/news/publications/ai-governance-around-world-uk
19 https://digital-strategy.ec.europa.eu/en/library/digital-omnibus-ai-regulation-proposal
20 https://www.compliancehub.wiki/metas-rejection-of-eu-ai-code-of-practice-implications-for-global-ai-compliance-frameworks/
21 https://blog.google/company-news/inside-google/around-the-globe/google-europe/eu-ai-code-practice/
22 https://aichampions.eu/
23 https://www.foreignaffairs.com/united-states/ai-divide

Chapter 8

1 https://journals.plos.org/plosone/article?id=10.1371/journal.pone.0286529
2 https://www.infoq.com/articles/agile-UK-government/
3 https://www.gov.uk/service-manual/technology/moving-away-from-legacy-systems
4 https://pmc.ncbi.nlm.nih.gov/articles/PMC8685936/
5 https://public.digital/pd-insights/blog/2018/04/public-digital-the-strategy-of-delivery
6 https://www.ft.com/content/6bfea441-e16c-499a-a887-69f735c29389

Bibliography

General further reading

Agrawal, Ajay, Joshua Gans and Avi Goldfarb. 2018. *Prediction Machines: The Simple Economics of Artificial Intelligence*. Boston: Harvard Business Review Press.

Agrawal, Ajay, Joshua Gans and Avi Goldfarb. 2022. *Power and Prediction: The Disruptive Economics of Artificial Intelligence*. Boston: Harvard Business Review Press.

Brown, Alan. 2019. *Delivering Digital Transformation: A Manager's Guide to the Digital Revolution*. De Gruyter.

Brown, Alan. 2021. *Digital Economy Dispatches: Critical Reflections on How to Succeed with Digital Transformation in Turbulent Times*. Unities Press.

Brown, Alan. 2024. *Surviving and Thriving in the Age of AI: A Handbook for Digital Leaders*. London Publishing Partnership.

Brown, Alan, Jerry Fishenden and Mark Thompson. 2014. *Digitalizing Government: Understanding and Implementing New Digital Business Models*. Basingstoke: Palgrave Macmillan.

Crawford, Kate. 2021. *Atlas of AI: Power, Politics, and the Planetary Costs of Artificial Intelligence*. New Haven: Yale University Press.

Fishenden, Jerry. 2023. *Fracture: The Collision Between Technology and Democracy – and How We Fix It*. Independently published.

Greenway, Andrew, Ben Terrett, Mike Bracken and Tom Loosemore. 2023. *Digital Transformation at Scale: Why the Strategy Is Delivery*. London Publishing Partnership.

Larson, Erik J. 2021. *The Myth of Artificial Intelligence: Why Computers Can't Think the Way We Do*. Belknap Press.

Narayanan, Arvind, and Sayash Kapoor. 2024. *AI Snake Oil: What Artificial Intelligence Can Do, What It Can't, and How to Tell the Difference*. Princeton University Press.

Pope, Richard. 2023. *Platformland: An Anatomy of Next-Generation Public Services*. London Publishing Partnership.

Susskind, Richard. 2025. *How to Think about AI: A Guide for the Perplexed*. Oxford University Press.

Suleyman, Mustafa, and Michael Bhaskar. 2023. *The Coming Wave: Technology, Power, and the Twenty-first Century's Greatest Dilemma*. New York: Crown.

Chapter 1

Barbour, Sharon, Nat Wright and Aidan McNamee. 2024. NHS computer issues linked to patient harm. *BBC News*, 30 May (https://www.bbc.co.uk/news/articles/c4nn0vl2e780).

Baumann, Bill. 2021. Lessons learned from the NHS IT system failure. Blog Post, 19 May, Panorama Consulting (https://panorama-consulting.com/nhs-it-system-failure/).

Colt. 2025. Supporting AI in the UK: a whitepaper to government. White Paper, January, Colt Technology Services (https://www.colt.net/resources/insights/new-white-paper-outlining-steps-for-uk-to-accelerate-ai-as-a-growth-driver).

Department for Digital, Culture, Media and Sport. 2021. National AI strategy. Guidance Document, September, DCMS (https://www.gov.uk/government/publications/national-ai-strategy).

Department for Science, Innovation and Technology. 2023. A pro-innovation approach to AI regulation. White Paper, March, DSIT (https://www.gov.uk/government/publications/a-pro-innovation-approach-to-ai-regulation).

Department for Science, Innovation and Technology. 2025. Artificial intelligence playbook for the UK Government. Guidance

Document, February, DSIT (https://www.gov.uk/government/publications/ai-playbook-for-the-uk-government).

Department for Science, Innovation and Technology. 2025. AI opportunities action plan. Independent Report, January, DSIT (https://www.gov.uk/government/publications/ai-opportunities-action-plan).

Desklib. 2023. National Health Service system failure case study analysis. Blog Post, 21 May, Desklib (https://desklib.com/study-documents/nhs-system-failure-case-study/).

Faith, Becky, Kevin Hernandez and James Beecher. 2022. Digital poverty in the UK. Report, May, British Academy (https://www.thebritishacademy.ac.uk/publications/digital-poverty-in-the-uk/).

Harper, Richard H. R. 2025. *The Shape of Thought: Reasoning in the Age of AI*. McGill-Queen's University Press.

Henrico Dolfing. 2019. Case study 1: the £10 billion IT disaster at the NHS. Blog Post, 20 January, HenricoDolfing.com (https://www.henricodolfing.ch/en/case-study-1-the-10-billion-it-disaster-at-the-nhs/).

Justinia, Taghreed. 2017. The UK's National Programme for IT: why was it dismantled? *Health Services Management Research* 30(1): 2–9.

March, James G. 1994. *A Primer on Decision Making: How Decisions Happen*. Free Press.

National Audit Office. 2024. Use of artificial intelligence in government. NAO Report, March, Department for Science, Innovation and Technology (https://www.nao.org.uk/reports/use-of-artificial-intelligence-in-government/).

Nominet Digital Youth Index. 2024. Digital exclusion data, UK (https://digitalyouthindex.uk/).

Office for National Statistics. 2025. Young people not in education, employment or training (NEET), UK. Statistical Bulletin, August, ONS (https://www.ons.gov.uk/employmentandlabourmarket/peoplenotinwork/unemployment/bulletins/youngpeoplenotineducationemploymentortrainingneet/august2025).

Parliamentary and Health Service Ombudsman. 2024. Discharge from mental health care: making it safe and patient-centred. Report, February (https://www.ombudsman.org.uk/sites/default/files/Discharge%20from%20mental%20health%20care%20making%20it%20safe%20and%20patient-centred_10.pdf).

Pullen, Charlynne. 2023. Youth unemployment: lessons to learn. Report, Gatsby Foundation (https://www.gatsby.org.uk/app/uploads/sites/2/2025/07/youth-unemployment-report-v6.pdf).

Chapter 2

Bennett School of Public Policy. 2019. The rise and fall of UK digital government: learning from the past. Blog Post, 9 October, Bennett School of Public Policy, University of Cambridge (https://www.bennettschool.cam.ac.uk/blog/rise-and-fall-uk-digital-government/).

Cabinet Office and Central Digital and Data Office. 2022. Transforming for a digital future: 2022 to 2025 roadmap for digital and data. Policy Paper, June, Cabinet Office and Central Digital and Data Office (https://www.gov.uk/government/publications/roadmap-for-digital-and-data-2022-to-2025).

Centre for Data Ethics and Innovation. nd. Homepage. Department for Science, Innovation and Technology (https://www.gov.uk/government/organisations/centre-for-data-ethics-and-innovation).

Chartered Institute of Personnel and Development. 2023. Devolution and evolution in UK skills policy. Report, October, CIPD (https://www.cipd.org/uk/knowledge/reports/devolution-evolution-skills-policy/).

Competition and Markets Authority. 2021. Update on Open Banking. Corporate Report, November, CMA (https://www.gov.uk/government/publications/update-governance-of-open-banking/update-on-open-banking).

Davies, John, Joel Klinger, Juan Mateos-Garcia and Kostas Stathoulopoulos. 2020. The art in the artificial: AI and the UK creative industries. Report, June, Creative Industries Policy and Evidence Centre (https://pec.ac.uk/wp-content/uploads/2023/12/PEC-and-Nesta-report-The-art-in-the-artificial.pdf).

Department for Business and Trade. 2025. Industrial strategy: UK sector analysis. Policy Paper, June, DBT (https://www.gov.uk/government/publications/industrial-strategy).

Department for Digital, Culture, Media and Sport. 2022. UK digital strategy. Policy Paper, July, DCMS (https://www.gov.uk/government/publications/uks-digital-strategy).

Department for Education. 2024. Skills England: driving growth and widening opportunities. Report, September, DfE (https://www.gov.uk/government/publications/skills-england-report-driving-growth-and-widening-opportunities).

Energy UK. 2025. How AI is enhancing the energy system. Blog Post, 31 July (https://www.energy-uk.org.uk/publications/how-ai-is-enhancing-the-energy-system/).

Kattel, Rainer, and Ville Takala. 2023. The case of the UK's Government Digital Service: the professionalisation of a paradigmatic public digital agency. *Digital Government: Research and Practice* 4(4): Paper 28 (http://dx.doi.org/10.1145/3630024).

Monavate. nd. Zilch: redefining credit in an age of responsible lending (https://www.monavate.com/case-studies/redefining-credit-in-an-age-of-responsible-lending).

National Grid. 2025. National Grid and Emerald AI announce strategic partnership to demonstrate AI power flexibility in the UK. Press Release, 15 September (https://www.nationalgrid.com/national-grid-and-emerald-ai-announce-strategic-partnership-demonstrate-ai-power-flexibility-uk).

NHS England. nd. Transformation Directorate: digitise, connect, transform – guidelines for digitised healthcare (https://transform.england.nhs.uk/digitise-connect-transform/).

Office for National Statistics. 2023. UK digital economic research 2020. Article, 18 May, ONS (https://www.ons.gov.uk/economy/economicoutputandproductivity/output/articles/ukdigitaleconomicresearch/2020).

Poole, George. 2025. AI in the creative industries. Article, 29 October, Major Players (https://www.majorplayers.co.uk/insights/ai-in-the-creative-industries).

Responsible Finance. nd. Homepage and lending principles (https://responsiblefinance.org.uk/).

Ross, Matt. 2022. The rise and fall of GDS: lessons for digital government. Article, 9 July, Global Government Forum (https://www.globalgovernmentforum.com/the-rise-and-fall-of-gds-lessons-for-digital-government/).

Shead, Sam. 2020. How a computer algorithm caused a grading crisis in British schools. CNBC, 21 August (https://www.cnbc.com/2020/08/21/computer-algorithm-caused-a-grading-crisis-in-british-schools.html).

Statista. 2024. Digital economy in the United Kingdom (UK): statistics and facts (https://www.statista.com/topics/7208/digital-economy-in-the-uk/).

Walsh, Bryan. 2020. How an AI grading system ignited a national controversy in the UK. Article, 19 August, Axios (https://www.axios.com/2020/08/19/england-exams-algorithm-grading).

Wierzbicki, Stanislaw. 2025. Open Banking in the UK: adoption, impact, and future trends in 2025. Article, 7 July, Noda (https://noda.live/articles/open-banking-in-the-uk).

Chapter 3

Aldane, Jack. 2025. Skills gaps harming public sector AI adoption, warns UK spending watchdog. Article, 5 November, Global Government Forum (https://www.globalgovernmentforum.com/skills-gaps-harming-public-sector-ai-adoption-warns-uk-spending-watchdog/).

Cabinet Office. 2025. UK government resilience framework: strategic approach to resilience and prevention. Policy Paper, December, Cabinet Office (https://www.gov.uk/government/publications/the-uk-government-resilience-framework/the-uk-government-resilience-framework-html).

Cabinet Office. 2025. UK government resilience action plan: resilience capacity and cross-sector risks. Policy Paper, July, Cabinet Office (https://www.gov.uk/government/publications/uk-government-resilience-action-plan).

Central Digital and Data Office. 2023. Transforming for a digital future: 2022 to 2025 roadmap for digital and data. Policy Paper, November, CDDO (https://www.gov.uk/government/publications/roadmap-for-digital-and-data-2022-to-2025).

Centre for Data Ethics and Innovation. nd. Advice and reports on responsible AI (https://www.gov.uk/government/organisations/centre-for-data-ethics-and-innovation).

Cirri, Giulia. 2025. The State and Vision of digital government. Summary Document, February, Oxford Insights (https://oxfordinsights.com/insights/the-state-and-vision-of-digital-government/).

Davies, John, Joel Klinger, Juan Mateos-Garcia and Kostas Stathoulopoulos. 2020. The art in the artificial: AI and the UK creative industries. Report, June, Creative Industries Policy and Evidence Centre (https://pec.ac.uk/wp-content/uploads/2023/12/PEC-and-Nesta-report-The-art-in-the-artificial.pdf).

de Genot de Nieukerken, Nicolas, and Pierre Fournier. 2025. Three Open Banking use cases for unlocking smarter growth (case studies). Article, 25 July, SBS (https://sbs-software.com/insights/open-banking-use-cases-growth/).

Department for Business and Trade. 2025. SME Digital Adoption Taskforce: final report – financial barriers to digital and AI adoption. Independent Report, 31 July, DBT (https://www.gov.uk/government/publications/sme-digital-adoption-taskforce-final-report/sme-digital-adoption-taskforce-final-report).

Department for Science, Innovation and Technology. 2025. A blueprint for modern digital government: a long-term vision for digital public services, a six-point plan for reform, and the role of the new digital centre of government. Policy Paper, January, DSIT (https://www.gov.uk/government/publications/a-blueprint-for-modern-digital-government).

Digital Catapult. nd. Accelerating AI innovation in the West of England creative industries (case studies) (https://www.digicatapult.org.uk/case-studies/study/accelerating-ai-innovation-west-of-england-creative-industries/).

Harrington, Justin. 2025. AI in the UK public sector. Article, 12 June, LocalGovernmentLawyer.co.uk (https://www.localgovernmentlawyer.co.uk/information-law/344-information-law-features/61261-ai-in-the-uk-public-sector).

Hoskins, Joel. 2025. An old challenge in the new era: how the public sector can benefit from the age of AI. Productivity Insights Paper 060, Productivity Institute (https://www.productivity.ac.uk/wp-content/uploads/2025/09/PIP60-Old-Challenge-in-the-New-Era-September-2025.pdf).

Human Learning Systems. 2024. Adaptive management practice in the UK government. Case Study, Human Learning Systems (https://www.humanlearning.systems/uploads/7685%20CPI%20-%20FCDO%20case%20study%20V2-%20TL%20proof%20read%20version.pdf).

Marcus, Gary, and Ernest Davis. 2019. *Rebooting AI: Building Artificial Intelligence We Can Trust*. Vintage Books.

NHS. 2025. Artificial Intelligence. Guidance, April, NHS (https://transform.england.nhs.uk/information-governance/guidance/artificial-intelligence/).

NHS Confederation. 2025. NHS communications artificial intelligence operating framework. Guidance Document, 1 October (https://www.nhsconfed.org/publications/nhs-communications-artificial-intelligence-operating-framework).

NHS England. 2023. Inclusive digital healthcare: a framework for NHS action on digital exclusion. Framework, September, NHS England (https://www.england.nhs.uk/long-read/inclusive-digital-healthcare-a-framework-for-nhs-action-on-digital-inclusion/).

Office for National Statistics. 2025. Public opinions and social trends, Great Britain: August 2025 (trust in AI stats). Statistical Bulletin, 19 September (https://www.ons.gov.uk/people

populationandcommunity/wellbeing/bulletins/publicopinionsandsocialtrendsgreatbritain/august2025).

Open Banking Limited. 2025. AI and open finance: shaping the future of financial innovation. Article, 23 September (https://www.openbanking.org.uk/insights/ai-and-open-finance-shaping-the-future-of-financial-innovation/).

Skills England. 2025. Barriers to AI skills development. Research and Analysis, November (https://www.gov.uk/government/publications/ai-skills-for-the-uk-workforce/barriers-to-ai-skills-development).

Starmer, Keir. 2025. Prime Minister's remarks at London Tech Week 2025. Speech delivered on 9 June at Olympia, London (https://www.gov.uk/government/speeches/prime-ministers-remarks-at-london-tech-week-2025-monday-9-june).

Starmer, Keir. 2025. PM speech on AI Opportunities Action Plan. Speech delivered on 13 January at UCL East, London (https://www.gov.uk/government/speeches/pm-speech-on-ai-opportunities-action-plan-13-january-2025).

Tech South West/Kene Partners. 2025. Driving AI innovation through NEW proof-of-concept funding. Article, 22 August (https://www.techsouthwest.co.uk/driving-ai-innovation-funding/).

Tony Blair Institute for Global Change. 2025. What the UK thinks about AI: building public trust to accelerate adoption. White Paper, September, Tony Blair Institute for Global Change (https://institute.global/insights/tech-and-digitalisation/what-the-uk-thinks-about-ai-building-public-trust-to-accelerate-adoption).

Transform UK. nd. Mind the gap: overcoming the key barriers in NHS digital transformation. Blog Post, Transform UK (https://www.transformuk.com/our-thinking/insights/mind-the-gap-overcoming-the-key-barriers-in-nhs-digital-transformation/).

Whittaker, Tom. 2021. AI assurance and responsible innovation: Centre for Data and Ethics report. Article, 14 July, Burges Salmon (https://www.burges-salmon.com/articles/102h2wj/ai

-assurance-and-responsible-innovation-centre-for-data-and-ethics-report/).

Chapter 4

Civica. 2024. UK government reaches pivotal moment in its digital transformation: UK Digital Roadmap review (One Login, governance, collaboration, AI adoption). Report, October, Civica (https://www.civica.com/en-gb/news-library/uk-government-reaches-pivotal-moment-in-its-digital-transformation/).

Cornerstone Network. 2024. Cornerstone launches 6-point blueprint for UK digital infrastructure. Press Release, 15 May (https://www.cornerstone.network/policy-reform-blueprint-digital-transform/).

Department for Business and Trade. 2023. Design principles for inclusive smart data schemes: research conducted by Savanta on behalf of the Department for Business and Trade. Report, July, DBT (https://www.gov.uk/government/publications/design-principles-for-inclusive-smart-data-schemes).

Department for Education. nd. Accessibility and inclusive design manual (https://accessibility.education.gov.uk/).

Department for Science, Innovation and Technology. 2023. Digital Regulation: driving growth and unlocking innovation – policy overview and new regulatory approaches. Policy Paper, October, DSIT (https://www.gov.uk/government/publications/digital-regulation-driving-growth-and-unlocking-innovation/digital-regulation-driving-growth-and-unlocking-innovation).

Department for Science, Innovation and Technology. 2025. A blueprint for modern digital government. Policy Paper, January, DSIT (https://www.gov.uk/government/publications/a-blueprint-for-modern-digital-government/a-blueprint-for-modern-digital-government-html).

Foreign, Commonwealth and Development Office. 2017. Delivering institutional reform at scale: problem-driven approaches supported by adaptive programming. Synthesis Paper,

June, FCDO (https://www.gov.uk/research-for-development-outputs/delivering-institutional-reform-at-scale-problem-driven-approaches-supported-by-adaptive-programming).

Fox, Alex, and Chris Fox. 2024. The motivational state: a strengths-based approach to improving public sector productivity. Essay, November, Demos (https://demos.co.uk/wp-content/uploads/2024/11/The-Motivational-State_2024_Nov.pdf).

HM Government. 2023. Government Functional Standard: GovS – digital. Standards Document, December (https://www.gov.uk/government/publications/government-functional-standard-govs-005-digital).

Leone de Castris, Arcangelo, and Charlie Thomas. 2026. AI governance around the world: country profile – United Kingdom. Report, January, The Alan Turing Institute (https://www.turing.ac.uk/sites/default/files/2026-01/ai_governance_around_the_world_-_uk.pdf).

Restore. nd. A guide to digital transformation for government and councils (https://www.restore.co.uk/informationmanagement/resource-hub/insights/government-digital-transformation/).

Tony Blair Institute for Global Change. 2025. Governing in the age of AI: reimagining local government. White Paper, May, Tony Blair Institute for Global Change (https://institute.global/insights/politics-and-governance/governing-in-the-age-of-ai-reimagining-local-government).

Chapter 5

Department for Education. 2025. Lifelong learning entitlement: what it is and how it will work. Policy Paper, November, DfE (https://www.gov.uk/government/publications/lifelong-learning-entitlement-lle-overview/lifelong-learning-entitlement-overview).

Department for Education. 2025. Skills for jobs: lifelong learning for opportunity and growth. Policy Paper, January, DfE (https://assets.publishing.service.gov.uk/media/601980f2e90e07128a353aa3/Skills_for_jobs_lifelong_learning_for_opportunity_and_growth__web_version_.pdf).

Department for Science, Innovation and Technology. 2025. Digital inclusion action plan: first steps. Policy Paper, February, DSIT (https://www.gov.uk/government/publications/digital-inclusion-action-plan-first-steps).

Department for Science, Innovation and Technology. 2025. Plan to increase digital skills to deliver growth and opportunity for all. Press Release, 26 February (https://www.gov.uk/government/news/plan-to-increase-digital-skills-to-deliver-growth-and-opportunity-for-all).

Experis UK. 2025. Closing the digital skills gap: the 2025 talent shortage. Article, 19 March (https://www.experis.co.uk/blog/2025/03/closing-the-digital-skills-gap-the-2025-talent-shortage?source=google.com).

FutureDotNow. 2023. The UK workforce digital skills gap: why closing it matters and a roadmap for action. Report, July, FutureDotNow (https://futuredotnow.uk/wp-content/uploads/2023/07/FutureDotNow-roadmap_final-digital.pdf).

FutureDotNow. 2025. Lack of digital skills in workforce costing UK over £23 billion per year. Press Release, 6 May (https://futuredotnow.uk/lack-of-digital-skills-in-workforce-costing-uk-over-23-billion-per-year/).

Good Things Foundation. 2025. Digital services: expert overview – August 2024. Policy Paper, January, Good Things Foundation (https://www.goodthingsfoundation.org/policy-and-research/what-works-colab/digital-services-briefing).

Greater Manchester Combined Authority. 2024. Greater Manchester Digital Blueprint 2023–26 (https://www.greatermanchester-ca.gov.uk/what-we-do/digital/digital-strategy/).

IUK Business Connect. 2025. Building a digitally confident, AI-ready workforce. Article, 24 July (https://iuk-business-connect.org.uk/news/building-a-digitally-confident-ai-ready-workforce/).

ManpowerGroup UK. 2025. UK labour market: it's not a digital skills gap, it's a chasm. Report/White Paper, July, ManpowerGroup UK (https://www.manpowergroup.co.uk/b_uk-labour-market-its-not-a-digital-skills-gap-its-a-chasm/).

Office for National Statistics. 2019. Exploring the UK's digital divide – who lacks digital skills and why. Article, March, ONS (https://www.ons.gov.uk/peoplepopulationandcommunity/householdcharacteristics/homeinternetandsocialmediausage/articles/exploringtheuksdigitaldivide/2019-03-04).

Prime Minister's Office. 2025. PM launches national skills drive to unlock opportunities for young people in tech. Press Release, 8 June (https://www.gov.uk/government/news/pm-launches-national-skills-drive-to-unlock-opportunities-for-young-people-in-tech).

TechUK. 2022. Preparing the UK for the future of work. Report, September, TechUK (https://www.techuk.org/resource/preparing-the-uk-for-the-future-of-work.html).

WorldSkills UK. 2021. Disconnected: exploring the digital skills gap. Report, WorldSkills UK (https://www.worldskillsuk.org/insights/disconnected-exploring-the-digital-skills-gap/).

Chapter 6

Ada Lovelace Institute. 2022. Algorithmic impact assessment: a case study in healthcare. Report, February, Ada Lovelace Institute (https://www.adalovelaceinstitute.org/report/algorithmic-impact-assessment-case-study-healthcare/).

Centre for Data Ethics and Innovation. nd. Building trust and enabling ethical innovation in UK data and AI (https://www.gov.uk/government/organisations/centre-for-data-ethics-and-innovation).

Daniels, Rory. 2023. Institutions of innovation: Centre for Data Ethics and Innovation. Article, 18 October, techUK (https://www.techuk.org/resource/institutions-of-innovation-centre-for-data-ethics-and-innovation.html).

Department for Science, Innovation and Technology. 2024. Assuring a responsible future for AI. Report, November, DSIT (https://www.gov.uk/government/publications/assuring-a-responsible-future-for-ai).

Department for Science, Innovation and Technology. 2025. Implementing the UK's AI regulatory principles: initial guidance for regulators. Policy Paper, February, DSIT (https://www.gov.uk/government/publications/implementing-the-uks-ai-regulatory-principles-initial-guidance-for-regulators).

Fagleman, David. 2024. The UK's approach to AI in financial services risks another financial crisis. Blog Post, 10 December, Finance Innovation Lab (https://financeinnovationlab.org/the-uks-approach-to-ai-in-financial-services-risks-another-financial-crisis/).

Future Work APPG. 2025. How is AI impacting the Creative Industries? Meeting Minutes, 5 June (https://www.futureworkappg.org.uk/news/creative-industries-appg).

Gallo, Valeria, and Suchitra Nair. 2024. The UK's framework for AI regulation. Article, 21 February, Deloitte (https://www.deloitte.com/uk/en/blogs/ecrs/the-uks-framework-for-ai-regulation.html).

Institute of Engineering and Technology. 2024. AI and sustainability policy position paper. Position Paper, November, IET (https://www.theiet.org/media/auwftwzk/ai-and-sustainability-policy-position-paper.pdf).

NHS England. nd. AI knowledge repository (https://digital.nhs.uk/services/ai-knowledge-repository).

Northumbria University. 2024. Researching ethical review to support Responsible AI in UK policing. Article, 6 February (https://www.northumbria.ac.uk/about-us/news-events/

news/researching-ethical-review-to-support-responsible-ai-in-policing/).

Shead, Sam. 2020. How a computer algorithm caused a grading crisis in British schools. CNBC, 21 August (https://www.cnbc.com/2020/08/21/computer-algorithm-caused-a-grading-crisis-in-british-schools.html).

Tabor, Francesca. 2025. Policy framework for sustainable AI in the UK. Policy Framework, May, FRANKI T (https://www.francescatabor.com/articles/2025/5/5/policy-framework-for-sustainable-ai-in-the-uk).

UK Finance. 2025. Generative AI in action: opportunities and risk management in financial services. Report, January, UK Finance (https://www.ukfinance.org.uk/policy-and-guidance/gen-ai-report).

University of Bristol. nd. The 2020 GCSE and A-level 'exam grades fiasco': analysis and scenario (https://www.bristol.ac.uk/cmm/research/grade/).

University of Cambridge/Bennett Institute. 2025. Forcing UK creatives to 'opt out' of AI training risks stifling new talent, Cambridge experts warn. Article, 20 February (https://www.cam.ac.uk/research/news/forcing-uk-creatives-to-opt-out-of-ai-training-risks-stifling-new-talent-cambridge-experts-warn).

Weizenbaum, Joseph. 1976. *Computer Power and Human Reason: From Judgment to Calculation*. W.H. Freeman.

Chapter 7

Baker, Richard. 2025. UK leadership in digital finance: building a standards-based future. Speech given to the Digital Markets and Digital Money APPG at the Evidence Session held on 2 September 2025 (https://tokenovate.com/uk-leadership-in-digital-finance).

Business.gov.uk. nd. Creative industries. Sector Overview (https://www.business.gov.uk/invest-in-uk/investment/sectors/creative-industries/).

Business.gov.uk. nd. Artificial intelligence (https://www.business.gov.uk/campaign/grow-your-business-in-the-uk/artificial-intelligence/).

Cavanaugh, Luke. 2024. UK bets big on AI-driven diplomatic services. Article, 19 November, GovInsider (https://govinsider.asia/intl-en/article/uk-bets-big-on-ai-driven-diplomatic-services).

Consultancy.uk. 2021. UK has 4th largest digital economy in the world. Article, 29 November (https://www.consultancy.uk/news/29700/uk-has-4th-largest-digital-economy-in-the-world).

Creative UK. 2023. The creative industries sector vision. Article, 14 June (https://www.wearecreative.uk/the-creative-industries-sector-vision2/).

Department of Health and Social Care. 2022. Genome UK: 2022 to 2025 implementation plan for England. Policy Paper, December, DHSC (https://www.gov.uk/government/publications/genome-uk-2022-to-2025-implementation-plan-for-england/).

Digital Catapult. 2021. New global index ranks UK first in Europe for advanced digital technology. Press Release, 20 September (https://www.digicatapult.org.uk/about/press-releases/post/new-global-index-ranks-uk-first-in-europe-for-advanced-digital-technology/).

Genomics England. nd. Genomics in the UK (https://www.genomicsengland.co.uk/genomic-medicine/genomics-in-uk).

HM Treasury. 2021. UK's global fintech leadership bolstered by new review. Article, 26 February, GOV.UK (https://www.gov.uk/government/news/uks-global-fintech-leadership-bolstered-by-new-review).

Ikhlaq, Usman, and Kir Nuthi. 2025. Industrial Strategy 2025: what does it mean for AI? Article, 25 June, TechUK (https://www.techuk.org/resource/industrial-strategy-2025-what-does-it-mean-for-ai.html).

Mayer, Hannah, Lareina Yee, Michael Chui and Roger Roberts. 2025. Superagency in the workplace: empowering people to unlock AI's full potential. Report, January, McKinsey (https://www.mckinsey.com/capabilities/tech-and-ai/our-insights/

superagency-in-the-workplace-empowering-people-to-unlock-ais-full-potential-at-work).

Organisation for Economic Co-operation and Development. 2024. OECD digital government index. Policy Paper, January, OECD (https://www.oecd.org/en/publications/2023-oecd-digital-government-index_1a89ed5e-en.html).

Organisation for Economic Co-operation and Development–Observatory of Public Sector Innoavtion. 2016. OECD Digital Government Toolkit. Guidance, OECD–OPSI (https://oecd-opsi.org/toolkits/oecd-digital-government-toolkit/).

Prabhu, Abhinaya. 2025. AI diplomacy in action: what does the OpenAI–UK deal really mean? Article, 22 July, Tech Funding News (https://techfundingnews.com/ai-diplomacy-in-action-what-does-the-openai-uk-deal-really-mean/).

Riley, Neal. 2025. Is the UK ready to be a global AI leader? Article, 20 October, Adaptavist (https://www.theadaptavistgroup.com/blog/is-the-uk-ready-to-be-a-global-ai-leader).

Tech Nation. 2025. UK AI sector spotlight 2025. Report, April, Tech Nation (https://technation.io/wp-content/uploads/2025/04/The-Tech-Nation-UK-AI-Sector-Spotlight-2025.pdf).

Wavestone. 2025. Global AI survey 2025: the paradox of AI adoption. Article, 14 October (https://www.wavestone.com/en/insight/global-ai-survey-2025-ai-adoption/).

Whitecap Consulting. 2025. AI for services 2025 report: unlocking opportunities in UK professional and financial services. Report, March, Whitecap (https://www.whitecapconsulting.co.uk/wp-content/uploads/2025/03/AI-for-Services-2025-report.pdf).

Chapter 8

ArvatoConnect. 2025. The UK Digital Transformation report: from deficit to delivery (https://www.arvatoconnect.co.uk/arvatotalks/the-uk-digital-transformation-report-from-deficit-to-delivery-public-sector/).

Cabinet Office. 2021. Organising for digital delivery. Independent Report, July, Cabinet Office (https://www.gov.uk/government/publications/organising-for-digital-delivery).

Cabinet Office. 2022. Continuous improvement assessment framework. Guidance Document, October, Cabinet Office (https://www.gov.uk/government/publications/continuous-improvement-assessment-framework).

Central Digital and Data Office. 2023. Transforming for a digital future: 2022 to 2025 roadmap for digital and data. Policy Paper, November, CDDO (https://www.gov.uk/government/publications/roadmap-for-digital-and-data-2022-to-2025).

Deloitte. 2023. UK falling behind rest of the world on realising value from new technology. Article, 23 November (https://www.deloitte.com/uk/en/about/press-room/uk-falling-behind-rest-of-the-world-on-realising-value-from-new-technology.html).

Department for Business and Trade. 2025. SME Digital Adoption Taskforce: final report. Independent Report, July, DBT (https://www.gov.uk/government/publications/sme-digital-adoption-taskforce-final-report).

Digital, Data and Technology Profession. 2023. The digital, data and technology playbook. Guidance Document, June, DDaT (https://www.gov.uk/government/publications/the-digital-data-and-technology-playbook).

Duus, Rikke, and Mike Cooray. 2016. The 5 barriers to effective digital transformation. Blog Post, 31 October, Chartered Management Institute (https://www.managers.org.uk/knowledge-and-insights/blog/barriers-to-digital-transformation/).

Harrison, Tom. 2016. The role of the centre in driving government priorities: the experience of 'delivery units'. Working Paper, July, Oxford Policy Management (https://www.opml.co.uk/sites/default/files/migrated_bolt_files/wp-role-centre-driving-government-priorities.pdf).

Infrastructure and Projects Authority. 2021. Transforming infrastructure performance: roadmap to 2030. Policy Paper, September, IPA (https://www.gov.uk/government/publications/transforming-infrastructure-performance-roadmap-to-2030).

Infrastructure and Projects Authority. 2024. The 7 lenses of transformation. Guidance Document, July, IPA (https://www.gov.uk/government/publications/7-lenses-of-transformation).

Kelly, Piers. 2023. Digital transformation case studies in the public sector. Article, 5 December, GovNet (https://blog.govnet.co.uk/technology/digital-transformation-case-studies-in-the-public-sector).

Local Government Association. 2024. Implementing digital social care records: case studies. Article, 17 December (https://www.local.gov.uk/case-studies/implementing-digital-social-care-records-case-studies).

The Manufacturer. 2025. Digital transformation in UK manufacturing: challenges and opportunities. Article, 20 January (https://www.themanufacturer.com/articles/digital-transformation-in-uk-manufacturing-challenges-and-opportunities/).

Index